PRAISE FOR *HUNTER OF HOPE*

In my opinion Ken has been dealt some brutal cards over the years. I admire the fight that he continues to show us all every day. Ken will tell you the truth no matter what. It's one of his strongest personality traits. Some of it you may want to hear, and some of it you may not. Some of it is just downright funny as hell. Sometimes I wonder what planet he's on. But all in all it's coming from the heart, his heart.
- Mark Calcavecchia, 13-time winner on the PGA Tour and the 1989 Open Championship

I first met Ken in the early 80s when I became his golf coach. In our 30-plus year relationship, there are plenty of highs and unfortunately, just as many lows. Ken was never one to be politically correct and could easily infuriate some people. As complicated as his life has been, I can tell you without hesitation, throughout everything, that he has always told the truth and he always had a huge heart. That's why I call him my friend. **- Peter Kostis, CBS Golf Analyst**

There are probably not a lot of men in this world who would be able to handle all the things that have happened to Ken Green, but with his determination he has fought his way through them. He is a character with a sense of humor and is not shy about speaking his mind-sometimes saying things that might make some shake their heads, and others just laugh. But he's always brutally honest about everything he says, and in what he believes in, and I am perfectly good with that! If I need a truthful opinion on something I always know where to get it! I'm honored to call him my friend! **- Larry Walker, 5-time MLB All-Star, National League MVP**

Ken Green Unleashed! Raw and unvarnished, Ken gives us a life so brutally honest, funny and tragic. A page-turner that reaches so many more than just us golfers! **- Maury Povich, talk show host and 4-handicap golfer**

HUNTER of HOPE

A Life Lived Inside, Outside, and On the Ropes

KEN GREEN

with Drew Nederpelt

N

NEWBERRY

Published in the United States by Newberry Funding, LLC. All rights reserved ©2019

Library of Congress Control Number available at KenGreenGolf.com

For personalized, signed copies of this book visit KenGreenGolf.com

For serial, film, foreign, or other rights, contact info@KenGreenGolf.com

This book was packaged by RocketShark Media RocketSharkMedia.com

ISBN: 978-0-578-49305-3

10 9 8 7 6 5 4 3 2 Printed in Canada

This book is dedicated to those souls who don't know they're not themselves, either through depression or life circumstances.

If you're struggling, never, ever give up.
Help will eventually arrive.

I promise.

CONTENTS

ACKNOWLEDGEMENTS

Being a rookie to the world of writing, much less book writing, I was told I must have an Acknowledgements section. What genius figured this out? I'm kind of rebelling against it, but I'm going to do it anyway. Therefore I'm a semi half-assed dope who is catering to the public relations department. Does this mean I actually learned something from Bean Demon and the PGA Tour?

The winner is my mom. Simple as that. She's the one who believed in me and sacrificed her last few decades for me. She's the one who loved me even after I broke her heart.

I will forever love my sister Shelley for forgiving me for being such a horse's ass.

How can I not say thank you to all my friends who stepped up to help me through all the disasters in my life- which are so many for one to have it's almost unbelievable.

I suppose I have to even thank the scumbags in Honduras for the two years of hell and then for me making a life-changing move.

I'm only able to give you these unbelievable stories because of a dog named Coco, who got help when she saw I was trying to end it all, so she must be thanked.

The real people I must say thanks to though are YOU, the reader. You are the ones who are going to make this book a success. You will tell a friend and from there we will get the real trickle-down-with-Green effect. Together we will unite. Together we are the ones who are going to help stop some disgusting behavior in our world. Be prepared to laugh and cry while you wonder how on earth this all happens to one man in one singular lifetime.

Wow, what genius came up with this Acknowledgement page theory again?

Brilliant, I say.

-KG

1/

"Mr. Green, Report to the Principal"

Age: 16
Legs: 2
Location: Nonnewaug High School, Woodbury, CT

I made a motion to grab the wheel of the car as my mom's head bobbed.

"Mom? *MOM!*"

"I got it baby, don't worry," said my mom as we pulled onto Minortown Road and coasted the 12-year-old Dodge Duster to the front of the blue-roofed Nonnewaug High School in Woodbury, Connecticut.

"Be more careful mom," I said as I grabbed my books from the back seat. After coming home from her third job as a waitress at the New Milford Diner, she typically fell asleep in her uniform and then three hours later changed for one of her two day-jobs, and off to school she drove me. I was very aware she was working her buns off to provide for her son, the wannabe professional golfer. I was also very well aware that showing up late literally three quarters of my days at school was less than ideal, but here we were.

I walked into school like I did most mornings; to empty hallways and a bare cafeteria. I went to my locker, and that's where Principal Stevens met me.

"Hey Mr. Green, glad to see you could make it today," he said.

I nodded, "Me too."

"Mr. Green, you know what? We've come up with a way for you to avoid being late for school," he continued, seemingly excited to share this new educational discovery with me.

"Yeah, how's that?" I said, legitimately interested in this groundbreaking innovation that would allow my mom not to have to work three jobs, or alternatively, to buy me a car so I could get to school on time.

"For every two days you're late, you will be forced to miss one golf match," he revealed.

It was a huge letdown. Not for me, but for my mom whom I was sure would be first in line to ensure I wasn't late to school again.

"Are you serious?" I asked, seriously.

"Yes, we are Mr. Green."

"No, I mean, are you *really* serious. Like dead serious?"

"Yes, we are. Effective immediately."

I nodded and did some quick arithmetic: I was already late about 75% of the time, and I only had 15 golf tournaments in a season, so I realized I would forfeit all of my matches if I was late 30 times, which, unless my mother was promoted to Executive Vice President of Diners or some such fantasy, was guaranteed.

"Okay, here you go," I said, handing my books to Principal Stevens.

"What are…you doing?" he asked, stepping back and letting the books crash to the ground.

"I'm done here," I said as I turned and walked out of Nonnewaug High School for the last time.

When my mom arrived home that afternoon I told her what had happened. She didn't have to tell me she supported my decision to quit school; she knew full well that she was already overextending herself to get me to school when she did, so we had no choice if I wanted to continue on my life's path, which brought her to the question she fully knew the answer to.

"Well, what are you going to do now?"

"I am going to play professional golf," said a cocky 16-year-old son to his already overburdened and overworked mother.

Looking back, it's clear my mother was a saint. Leave alone the fact that a responsible educator would have called my mother into school to see why Mr. Ken Green was perpetually late, and nine times out of ten, presented with the exact same scenario, a mother would have said '*Over my dead body,*' and waltzed their kid right back to that same school the next morning. But not Jane Marie Green. She had faith in her son, and probably more importantly, she knew that to argue with him was pointless.

I wasn't afraid of Principals or adults or authority. Even at my very young age I had been presented with obstacles far more severe than Principal Stevens, or anyone for that matter, could dream up in their wildest nightmares, and my mom knew it. I made a mental note to return to Nonnewaug High School after my first victory on the PGA Tour.

Alas, six years later, when I raised my first pro golf trophy, Nonnewaug High School was the furthest thing from my mind.

Green makes decision, leaves school to turn pro

October 1979

By Mark Schmiedel
News-Times sports staff

The question wasn't if. The question was when.

According to Ken Green, now is the time to make his move. The next time the Danbury golfer enters a tournament, he'll be teeing it up for money. At age 20, he is quitting college and turning pro.

He knew it would happen someday. Before he returned to the University of Florida Sept. 24, Green was trying to decide whether to stock out the whole of his final year of eligibility, or quit after the first semester and head for the Florida mini-tour. He stayed in Jacksonville just eight days before realizing his heart was no longer into college golf.

Green's disenchantment started last season when he, and several other Gator players, were upset with Coach John Darr's methods. When Green returned to school this fall, he found the situation hadn't changed. It made his decision that much easier.

"It just wasn't working out," said Green. "We got along, but we just never connected with the right ideas. I guess they were minor things, but because of the fact that I wasn't really interested in playing golf at the college level, I might have blown them all out of proportion. I guess I used that as an excuse to quit."

So Green is now back in Danbury, preparing to leave for Florida again. But instead of going to Jacksonville and the University of Florida, he'll head for Orlando and the Cypress Creek Country Club, site of his first pro venture.

Green will test the waters Marcia Dolan elected to pass up. Dolan, with one of the finest amateur records in the nation, thought briefly of turning pro. Instead, she chose marriage and a family. Dolan has had the best of both worlds, living the family life and continuing to win numerous tournaments. Her success has made Dolan a well-respected player up and down the East Coast.

In startling contrast, Green does not enjoy a wide reputation even in his home state. During this past

See GREEN, Page C-19

News-Times photo by Carol Kaliff

Ken Green . . . decided time was now

13

2/

The Masters

Through the years it seems that many have been left with the impression that I was not a fan of The Masters. That's dead wrong. I loved playing Augusta. What I did hate however were the powers in charge and their stuck-up attitudes thinking they were better than everyone else. Hord Hardin, Chairman of Augusta National and The Masters, was a "legendary autocrat" according to his *New York Times* obituary. He was the "Dick of Dicks" (apologies to Dicks everywhere) according to Ken Green's book.

My first Masters was 1986. We rented a house and I invited many of my friends to come enjoy the week. Truth be told I loved having them all there. The idea that I could give something back to my friends, something like watching The Masters from the inside, was very special to me. I was hitting the ball worse than a pig with a persimmon but in this game you just go out and see what happens. And so, in the first round, I had the greatest putting round in the history of The Masters, by far. In one day I had a total of three hundred feet of putts (a good day is anything over 100—which makes the average feet of putts made about 6 feet—*my average of putts made that round was 17 feet*). I made four putts from fifty feet that should've been a total of ten putts. I made four twenty-footers for par and a few more, ten or so, for more pars. So now I was leading The Masters, as a first-timer. It was a special day to be sure.

When I returned home to the place I was renting the neighbor had hung a huge banner across the street 60-feet-wide that read, "CONGRATULATIONS KEN GREEN FIRST ROUND LEADER

THE MASTERS." The guy must have owned a sign printing business because the thing was worth about two-grand in my estimation and while I'm totally worth a $2,000 sign, it wasn't something that I could imagine your average fan just going to Kinkos for. It was an incredible sight.

In the media tent I was a big hit due to the fact that I'm a talker and that my sister Shelley was on the bag- the first female caddy at Augusta, which, considering they wouldn't let women into the club for more than a decade and a half, makes me the first feminist on the PGA Tour. Bruce Berlet, a former Hartford writer and one of the best reporters in the business, tells me I was handling things perfectly until the dreaded question: "As this is your first Masters, can you tell us your impressions of Magnolia Lane?" They were speaking of the long, magnolia-tree festooned entrance to the venerable golf club.

I looked around and gave an honest answer: "It's not that impressive, really. There are a thousand roads and Sunday drives in Connecticut that are much prettier."

Now, call me crazy (and many do), but if you want to ask me a question with the expectation that I'm going to lie to you, then why ask your question in the first place? Just put what you want me to say in my mouth and claim I said it. To this day I don't understand people who get upset when people are honest with them. If someone tells me to come see their baby and they say, "Isn't he just the most precious baby you've ever seen?" I might say, "Oh yeah," but I'm equally liable to say, "Nope." Again, if you want me to lie to you, don't ask the question. If I tell you the truth, and you get upset, then that says more about you than it does me.

With their chins still on the ground, one of the reporters managed to ask me how I would handle the pressure of leading after the first round of my first Masters. Again, honesty prevailed: "I'm playing like a toilet plunger and I have no chance." While that was in fact the truth, what I really wanted to say was that I was going to hold back so Jack Nicklaus could win his last Masters. But that would have sent Augusta National into a green-blazered meltdown, so I refrained. It turns out Jack didn't need my help anyway, winning his 18th Major in an incredible come-from-behind round of 65 on Sunday that included a nice little 30 on the back nine. I was delighted that my hero had won the tournament I had led on day one.

One year I had our kids, Brad and Brooke, caddie for me in the Par-3 contest- which really meant they each just held a couple of clubs as we strolled the friendly confines of the par-3 course at Augusta that Wednesday. They were 6- and 4-years-old. They loved it and the crowd did too.

The next day I arrived at my locker for the first round and found a letter inside. I opened it slowly and saw it was from the head of The Masters, the aforementioned Mr. Hardin. The letter said, 'The Masters frowns upon children on the golf course' and told me in no uncertain terms not to allow the kids to caddie again. Poor Hord wasn't aware that if he wanted me to obey his wishes he probably should have worded the letter a little differently. The next year I did it again, and of course, I got another letter. And that was the beginning of The Masters tradition of having players' kids caddie for them at the par-3 contest, something that is very much encouraged at The Masters today. In fact, they even have little Masters caddie overalls made for each of the tykes. I have to believe that when I meet Hord again he will be greeting me at the Pearly Gates with another letter.

The 16th hole at Augusta is a pretty famous par-3. From Jack draining his 45-footer in 1975 to Tiger's incredible slow-roll chip-in that is replayed about every six minutes on Golf Channel, the hole has been a centerpiece of The Masters. Standing on the tee, there is water in front and to the left of the green. It's a perfect skip-shot opportunity. I convinced my pal Mark Calcavecchia to hit skip-shots on that hole-if either of us skipped it once and landed it on the green we owed the other guy $100. If you skipped it twice it was $200. Once again the crowd loved it and it brought some unique fun to the day. I got a letter in my locker for that, too. I never stopped doing it. Today, if a player doesn't try and skip it up to 16, they're booed. So those traditions you now see at Augusta, you can blame your friend Ken "Locker Letters" Green.

While I never intentionally tried to piss Hord off, I simply had a knack for it. Another year at the tournament and I was playing well—5-under through 11, when my name popped up on the leaderboard in the clubhouse. Famed golf teacher and CBS golf analyst Peter Kostis was having lunch right next to Hord when Hord turns to him, not knowing Peter was a close friend and my teacher, and said, "That Green is a pain in my ass." Too bad Hord's not around to see that Green actually created two of the most memorable traditions at his tournament. You're welcome Hord.

For the 1989 Masters the plan was to play at Harbour Town the week before so my wife Ellen could meet us at Augusta on Tuesday with the kids. The Masters had sent eight family tickets to the house, which Ellen was going to bring with her when she flew down from Connecticut. I was going to buy another eight, which was the max you could get, when I arrived. Ellen and I had some disagreement which turned into a blow-out. She decided she wasn't going to come to the tournament.

"Okay," I said, "if that's what you want, so be it, just overnight the tickets because I have half your family here."

She refused.

Her siblings and some of my friends tried to convince her otherwise, but they had as much luck as I did. Now it's Wednesday and we're all pretty sure we're not going to see those eight tickets. And securing eight tickets for the second most difficult sporting event in the country to get tickets for (Final Four being No. 1) was not an inconsiderable feat.

So, thinking outside the box, I came up with a genius idea. I'm going to go into the office and talk to Hord Hardin personally. I decide that instead of making up some BS story about lost or damaged tickets, I'm going to tell him the truth, thinking even he would understand the wrath of a wife, right?

I laid out my story, thinking I had done a masterful job of explaining my predicament. His answer was as shocking as it was simple: "You need to get better control of your wife. There are no more tickets for you."

Oopsy-shit, that didn't go over like I hoped. The others pleaded with Ellen once again and once again she refused to send the tickets. So the only thing we could do was try to sneak everybody in and hope no one got caught.

I decided we would arrange the troops by age—the younger ones (including Ellen's brothers) would go in without credentials, the plan being that they would be best physically equipped to move around quickly if questioned—the *Those Darn Kids* strategy.

So the next morning I dropped everybody off near the gate and then slowly drove back and forth bringing everyone in. I didn't give it too much thought when I got back from playing and found out that one of Ellen's brothers had been caught. But he had panicked and told them he was there with Ken Green, so they knew I was sneaking everybody into the damn Masters. He apologized and then he called

Ellen, thinking she'll certainly overnight the passes now. Not on your life. Instead she yelled at me for not giving her brothers a ticket.

The next day we're going to try the same trick. This time, on the way in, despite the fact that I waved my special Masters player's pass, they stopped the car like we were crossing into East Berlin in 1973. They wanted to see the badges of each of the people in the car. They made notes as to who was in the car, their names and badge numbers. As they were doing human inventory I'm sitting there wondering how we were going to sneak the others in who were still outside waiting for me.

I dropped off Round One and collected their tickets to transfer to those still waiting outside. Then we headed back out. This time we're hiding people everywhere- some are laying on others' feet in the back with blankets over them, while others are snuggling with my clubs in the trunk of the nice big Cadillac courtesy car. It was like an ironic underground railroad into Augusta National. We managed to pull off this stunt all four days. They even stopped and inventoried Calc's car, knowing he and I were best friends. And through it all I still had a job to do- play and compete in The Masters Tournament. Ironically I had my best Masters, finishing tied for tenth. Hord won a battle or two, but in the end, Greeny won the war.

My last Masters was in 1997 and once again I had a ton of friends fly down for the tournament. The night before the first round a bunch of them were outside the rental home playing hoops when I walked out to observe the talentless crew. At some point between the rainbow-airballs, triple-dribbles, and diabetes/asthma inhaler time-outs, the ball rolled under the car in the driveway, so of course I just reached under the car to grab it for them. My Connecticut buddy Doug Ramey, who was just walking out of the house, kiddingly gave me a bump on the ass. Little did he know I was just then reaching for the ball and my thumb hit it, breaking my thumb. Since I'm sure you're curious, the ball was just fine.

The next day I played awful and shot 87, but I blame only myself. I was going to withdraw because it was pointless to try to play a pro golf event with a bum hand. Then I found out that I was paired with the King, Arnold Palmer, for the second round. Arnold is a legend and a hero of mine and this was my first and only time I would ever play with him. There was no way I was quitting now!

The next day I had one of, if not my best day ever, on a golf course. Arnold was an absolute joy to play with. He told me stories that were just classics, and so funny. He even answered my wacky question about the most famous woman he'd ever had the pleasure of spending a night with. The name he revealed is something I will never repeat to anyone, even after his passing (Palmer died in 2016 at the age of 87). I gave him my word I wouldn't tell anyone and he trusted me with some delicate stories that I'll never divulge, even though I would love to tell someone. Never let it be said that I can't be discrete!

The Augusta weather was perfect that day. When we were on the 14th hole I realized I will probably never, ever have another chance to have a beer with the King. As I walked up the 14th I sent my friend Ertz to the concession to buy a beer, which he gave me as we teed off on 15. I then walked up to Arnie and said, "Arnie, this has been an absolute blast and I'll never have a better chance to have a beer with you, so I salute you." He looked at me and said, "You should've brought me one." I would have never presumed I could just bring the King a beer, but I love that he said it. For that I was initially fined, but I had my buddy Ertz write a letter claiming the beer was of the non-alcoholic variety, and the fine was rescinded. I can attest today however, there was nothing alcohol-free about that beer.

The media, knowing I would certainly have something to say after the round, was all over us when we finished. I told them how much fun I'd had and that I even had a chance to have a beer with the King. I told them my Masters had been a delight. They soaked it all in and thought it was a wonderful story. I then mentioned how lucky I was that it seemed like every time I played with a superstar, something weird and unique happened. They asked me to explain, so I expounded thusly:

In 1989 I was paired with Seve Ballesteros in the final round at Augusta. We were semi in the hunt but clearly needed a brilliant round to catch the leader, Ben Crenshaw. Seve played a masterful front nine. He hit each shot perfectly and made five birdies. It was a brilliant nine and he was now tied for the lead. The tough 10th hole was next- a hard right-to-left hole that requires a nice draw to get the maximum roll-out for a closer approach shot. Seve over-cooked his tee shot, hooking it along the tree line on the left side. When we arrived at our balls I was curious to see if he was going to have a shot, so I casually strolled over to the left side to take a peek. I got to his ball and saw he was in a little rut where he would have no chance to get a 2- or 3-iron (we didn't have high-trajectory hybrids in those days) up quickly enough to clear the top of the rut. I continued to my ball.

Standing by my ball, waiting for him to pitch out, I was shocked to see him taking a drop. I'm like *What the hell is that all about?* I then hustled my skinny tuchas back up that steep-ass hill in record time. I got there and asked the tournament official why Seve was getting a free drop (meaning he was allowed to pick up his ball and remove it from the rut with no penalty). To their credit, The Masters has an official on every hole for just these scenarios. This particular official explained to me that, "Here at Augusta we have a local rule where if we feel your lie is being affected by crowd damage, you get a free drop."

I was keenly aware of this rule because on the par-5 second hole I hit my second shot 20 yards right of the green into the "patrons," as they're called. Now, the day before it had poured rain so the area was basically all mud with heel prints all over the place. My ball was in one of those ruts when I was told that the heel print that my ball was sitting in was not "crowd damage." I am assuming even the birds at Augusta are well heeled patrons who wear shoes and boots. My reputation had gone so far as to reach the on-hole officials, who were all USGA, PGA of America, and R&A officials. Lord Hord strikes again!

Seve had a pure hardpan lie with zero crowd damage. Hell, the gallery wasn't even allowed to walk over there. I insisted on a second opinion. Keep in mind that golf is a game where the players are expected to self-police. However, when a player isn't self-policing sufficiently, it's incumbent on his playing partner(s) to stand up for the rest of the field. It was my job to guard the integrity of the scores out there, and that's what I did.

At this point we have an army following us since Seve is tied for the lead. We're just standing there waiting for another official when Seve says to me, "You can go now Ken, it's not like I'm going to cheat."

Without missing a beat I turned to him and said, "I'm not sure about that Seve. I'll wait."

The crowd moaned with *ooh's* and *aah's*. There was silence between us until the chief official, Michael Bonallack of the R&A, arrived. Before he even got to within 10 feet of the ball he pointed to Seve and said, "Put it back."

Seve was just being Seve; pure intimidation served with

heaps of Spanish charisma. Seve was a phenomenal golfer but he just couldn't help playing games on the course. I'm guessing it was a throwback to his hustling back in his early days and while I did the same when I played with friends, I would never play head-games with my peers. He would use intimidation to get favorable rulings that other players would have blanched at. He would often move when his playing partner was preparing to hit. He also tended to develop a sudden cough, and change-jingling was routine for him. I'm sure he was a great friend off the course, but on the course he was El Dickhead.

As it turned out, Seve and I both faded and neither of us won that Masters. Looking back, I'm honored to have played The Masters, and I'm even more psyched that I started two trends that players are all doing today. I'm waiting to see my Ken Green logo on all the kids' caddie bibs but I especially can't wait to see a plaque in my honor right next to the skip-zone on 16. Maybe I'll see how they're coming along with that when I see Hord again.

THE MASTERS SHOULD BE DEMOTED AS A MAJOR

Enough is enough. It's time for one of the most exciting golf tournaments to be demoted as a major championship. The Masters is great but the idea that there are guys being elevated as great Hall of Famers because they won at Augusta is just wrong. I'm going to list why The Masters needs to be given a new status, maybe *Holy Shit It's The Masters!*

The world of being a major champion means it's supposed to be hard to win. The exact opposite happens at Augusta. There are eight winners who have won the masters three times or more since 1935, its first year. The Players Championship doesn't have but one, Jack Nicklaus. The British Open would be next and that, too, is because of limited fields, but not as bad as The Masters.

Don't forget, before 1935 the Open rarely was visited by American players. So even though there are eight players who have won it three times or more, four of them won their three Opens before Yanks started playing regularly. The strong-field Open didn't truly start until the early 2000s when both organizations finally kissed and made up. Tiger is really the only guy who won it three times with great fields. The U.S. Open and the PGA Championship have only three each. That's not counting the players who have won twice at Augusta vs. other majors.

Augusta National, *the course like no other*, is perfectly set up for a certain style of golfer. It's as simple as that. How can we call it a major when you only have 90 some-odd golfers playing in it and most of them have absolutely zero chance of winning?

The Masters will never have a 9th alternate like John Daly (the PGA) from out of nowhere who wins, or even a Todd Hamilton (The Open Championship), or the Michael Campbells (U.S. Open), of the world who basically stun the golfing world despite being good golfers on tour when they won. It's really hard to win The Masters if you're not there. Jack Nicklaus is responsible for giving The Masters the ultimate major status. The early Masters' were yesteryear's version of today's World Golf Championship events.

Those who say *Well, those are the best players in the world so it's extremely hard to win,* have forgotten one simple fact: When the field is reduced you allow the great players a chance to win with their B or their C game because the week only allows for a few guys or so who play well.

Just do the numbers: Let's say that in any given tournament 10% of the starting field has a chance to win. Now let's apply those metrics to The Masters versus another major.

MASTERS: 85 entries, minus at least 40 who have no chance, leaves just five players competing at the end (10 percent of the initial, serious field). That allows great players like Jack or Tiger to contend with a shaky game.

US OPEN: Take 156 players and throw out 40 who are doomed, you now have 12 (10 percent of the initial, serious field) who will play well and be around on Sunday. That's seven extra players who are playing well that the studly Jack or Tiger now have to beat with their B or C game.

Now, that may not seem like a big difference, five guys versus 12 guys, but those extra seven professional golfers are playing great golf, and you can see how it becomes a very different equation. The Masters is the most exciting event pro golf has to offer, but it doesn't stay true to the real meaning of a major.

I actually have a few other reasons why The Masters needs to be demoted but I'm not going to waste your time with little points when I've clearly made my case. The Masters is the most exciting tournament but shouldn't be a major.

On the other hand, The Players Championship is the hardest event to win, period. It's also played on the same course, with almost equal excitement in finishes as to what Augusta has given us. Once again, my hero Jack Nicklaus, is a huge factor as to why that event never made it to the so-called major level, which I outline in Chapter 15.

Green buries the field

3/

They Said I Couldn't Do It

The year 1985 wasn't exactly going the way I had hoped heading into the summer. I had lost my sponsors and was now bankrolling my own travel on tour (thanks in part to my last-minute miracle of hitting 23 of 24 college basketball games with my friendly neighborhood bookie) and while I was now divorced from my first wife with most of my issues in the rearview mirror, money was still tighter than a fish's ass and I was still winless on the PGA Tour.

A month or so before the Buick Open that year, I called one of my best friends, Colonel Jack Gaddy, whom I had met on a golf course when I was 15-years-old. He was now living in Georgia but we chatted often about my golf and the tour. He inquired as to whether I was going to play the Houston Open in a few weeks. I told him I was committed to play but wasn't going to go. After significant prodding he managed to learn I wasn't going due to lack of funds. He immediately offered me $5,000, which I didn't want to take because he wasn't exactly loaded, but he loved me and believed enough in me that he was willing to give away some of his life savings. So I went to Houston and had my best tournament in eons. I made enough there to keep me playing for the rest of the year. Colonel got his $5,000 back after that Houston Open. He will always be one of my most prized and cherished friends.

At the end of July I had a week break so I decided to play in the

Connecticut Open at the New Haven Country Club. It was there that I won my first event in a long time. I played especially great down the stretch, which helped with confidence. As we all know, 96 percent of golf is in your head.

Two weeks later I arrived in Grand Blanc, Michigan, for the Buick Open at Warwick Hills Country Club. I started the first hole with a dumb-ass bogey when suddenly the horn blew to bring us all off the course due to an incoming storm. It was a three-hour delay and eventually I got tired of just hanging around listening to guys tell stories. So I went into the locker room and promptly fell asleep on a wooden bench. I was out like a light when suddenly a locker room attendant is shaking my shoulder.

"Sir, sir, do you know they're about to restart?" he said, looking at me like I was a lost puppy.

"Damn!" I jumped up and ran out to the second tee just in time. I managed to fire off a 67 that day, playing a shot I had lost since working with my longtime coach, Peter Kostis, who today is a CBS commentator. Peter and I had worked hard on hitting a little fade (a la Jack Nicklaus) but today every shot was curving right to left- a baby draw. I was perplexed as to why this was happening. It was a remarkable feat, one that I have never heard anyone else claim. I just accepted it and started aiming just right of the pin while still trying to hit a fade. So I'm literally aiming to the right of the target, and trying to hit a ball that goes further right. And the ball went left. Every. Single. Time.

The second day, still playing the opposite-shot game, I fired off a 69, which put me in very good shape but not leading. The third round things went really well—I shot an amazing 65, still using the opposite-shot approach.

At this point I'm tied with Wayne Grady of Australia (a future major champion). I was playing in my very first "last group on Sunday." I was pumped but still knew I had work to do. Shelley was caddying for me so we were getting good publicity, as she was the very first full-time female caddie on the PGA Tour and a beautiful girl to boot. My mom and my girlfriend Cathy flew out because my mom said she knew I was going to win.

Despite my mom's confidence, my only goal was simple: By the end of the day have the lowest score I could, regardless of how I achieved it. Grady had a great front nine and at the turn was three under and leading me by two shots. I wasn't out of it yet so I just kept thinking *attack, attack, attack.*

The 11th hole was a par-3 where I overcooked my shot to the left and missed the green. I had a difficult chip that had to land perfectly to stop it close to the hole. It was then that my magical sand wedge, the Shamrock, decided it would instead send the ball to the bottom of the cup for a birdie 2. I then went on to birdie the next few holes and next thing I knew I was standing on 17 with a four-shot lead. I told myself to stay focused because birdie-birdie by Grady and bogey-bogey by me would mean a four-shot swing in no time. I parred 17, as did Wayne.

So now I'm four up with one to go. Contrary to what some might think, I'm smart enough to know that the only way I can lose this tournament is if I hit it left and go out-of-bounds. So, being overly cautious, I proceed to hit it dead right into the adjacent fairway. I had a bunch of trees to get around and over. I'm thinking if Grady gets a birdie-a very real possibility- I can still win this with a double-bogey.

I then chunked my 4-iron short and left of the green. Now I'm getting nervous because I know I've got this- *or do I?*

In my perplexed state I lay the sod over my pitch shot and it ends up 45 feet short. I now have four putts to win, but from 45 feet, that's not a foregone conclusion.

I'm still in control, I tell myself, as I stand over my 45-foot putt. I look up towards the hole to see the outline of Shelley holding the pin for me since I can't see the hole. I am also blinded by the sun. In the ancient days of golf we didn't yet have electronic scoreboards. Instead we had the massive scoreboards you see at The Masters and the Memorial, where each score is posted by the hole. It was getting late and the sun was shining hard directly into my face, right through the hole in the scoreboard where my score for the 18th hole was going to be! I couldn't believe the symbolism. I'm putting for my first PGA Tour victory, I've made a mess of it so far, I'm standing over a putt that could put me into the rarified air of winners on tour, and shining bright as the brightest daylight, right into my eyes for my putt, is the sun, shining through the hole where, in a few minutes, they will blot out the sun with my score. Karma? Irony? Symbolism? Milli Vanilli? You decide, I have a putt to make.

I literally couldn't see the flag or the hole, much less figure out the break of the green. I knew it went left to right but had no clue how much. I elected to just hit the ball at Shelley with my typical *What could go wrong?*

I hit the putt and waited what seemed like an hour when the crowd erupted into an immense roar. It had gone in the damn hole! My hands went high in the air with a smile I would be hard pressed to replicate today. It was more out of *Wow, are you kidding me?* than, *Wow, I won*! I was in shock as day turned into a celebratory night, knowing I had pulled off a victory on the PGA Tour. A victory hitting nothing but confusing double-crosses. Me, a little nobody from Danbury, Connecticut, had won on the PGA Tour. I didn't sleep a wink that night, thinking a lot about others' faith in me that was directly responsible for this victory. While golf is a solitary sport, it's certainly a team effort.

The next day I flew to the Catskills in New York because I had committed to play in a friend's charity pro-am. Now, most players who win a tournament on the PGA Tour typically beg out of their Monday commitment. But I always kept my word and that year was no different, my first PGA Tour title notwithstanding.

4/

Gator Attack!

Age: 45
Legs: 2
Dog: Nip

It was your typical Florida day: sunshine and more sunshine. I played a round of golf at Bear Lakes in West Palm Beach and after we finished we had a cocktail and then I went home to my house on Antietam Lane, named after the bloodiest civil war battle ever, I learned from Lanny Wadkins one year. (I'm guessing all the roads in that development will now have to be renamed because they're all civil war battles, if the whack-a-doodles on the left get their way that is.) When I got home my dog Nip was psyched because that meant it was ball time.

My yard was small but good for us. It was your basic 7 yards by 30 yards. Nip ran down to the end of the yard where she thought I was going to throw the ball. When she got there I threw her a fastball with the racquet ball we used. It was a bullet and she jumped high enough to get it but it hit her front canine teeth and went flying over the fence and into the middle of a filthy canal about forty yards away. She looked at me and I at her.

I then snapped my fingers, which meant she was allowed to go get the ball. She ran back to me and then took off for the fence, clearing the 4-foot obstacle with ease. She kept running full speed into the canal and did an amazing doggy flop with a big splash. One second later I heard another splash.

Damn don't let that be what I think it is, I thought, terrified. I had seen one gator in all my 17-years on that canal, and it was a three-footer, and this did not sound like a three-footer. I bolted out of the gate and ran to the edge of the canal where I immediately saw Nip swimming back with the ball in her mouth, not a worry in the world. I also saw a big-ass gator swimming toward her at an angle which meant he was going to cut her off before Nip could reach land. My first thought was that I had to do something, and that first something was to run and jump on the gator.

I waited and watched, hoping the gator would miss her. I'm not sure what the chances are of alligators missing 100lb German Shepherds in the water, but it was proven to be pretty low in this instance, because when the gator got to Nip there was a huge splash and Nip was gone in a blink.

Oh no you don't, I thought, as I jumped into the canal and was suddenly neck-deep in putrid water. The water was still- no sign of Nip or the gator. *Shouldn't there be thrashing?* I wondered.

Wtf Green, why did you wait so long? I thought to myself. As I scanned the water and listened for any sounds of my poor Nip, I was pissed at myself. *You idiot, you should have done something,* I thought.

A minute passed. Then suddenly, twenty feet to my right the gator's tail and back pop out of the water. I purposefully and deliberately waddled myself over to the alligator, just a few inches away from the gator's back right leg and fat gut. The gator was drowning Nip. I thought for a few seconds and realized the gator's stomach was so fat I had no chance grabbing it there. I looked at its back foot and I'm telling you it was massive and way bigger than any gator claw I've ever seen or even knew about.

Just do it, just do it.

I grabbed onto the meaty end of the tail and punched the alligator's gut as hard as I could. Immediately the gator let go of what was left of Nip and swung that killer mouth around so that all I could see was a gaping maw full of white teeth staring at me. *Fuck.*

We then went into the "death roll" that gators are known for. I'd like to tell you I held on for a long time but I have no idea how long I held on until I popped up out of the water to see the gator about fifteen feet away, just looking at me. Nip was trying to swim back to shore so I took off after her. I'm guessing the gator was so shocked that it was now the hunted that he didn't come back after me.

I got to Nip and she was bleeding all over the place. I picked her up and ran to the car and drove to the emergency vet clinic faster than you need to know. When the vets finally came out they told me that they had stopped all the bleeding and she had about twenty-five stitches. She had a massive amount of water still in her and they weren't sure if she would live.

"Does she have a chance?" I asked the doctor.

"Yes, but not a good one," came the answer.

I said, "You don't know her, she'll live."

Two days later Nip was home and well. I, meanwhile, in case you're curious, had cut marks all over my body from my gator death roll and bruised ribs up the wazoo. Two days later Nip was ready to play ball. People would call and ask *How's Nip doing you dumb-ass?* She's doing great, don't worry about me guys. I couldn't play golf for six weeks but they wanted to know if Nip was okay. I love my friends, I tell you.

Three things went in our favor that day or neither of us would have made it out alive. The first was that the gator jumped into the water and made a loud splash. If he had just slithered in, or had already been in the water, by the time I realized Nip wasn't around, she would've been dead. The next thing was that the gator grabbed Nip right behind her front feet and right in front of her back feet. Anywhere else and she would've been death-rolled to doggy heaven.

The third thing was that the gator didn't come back after me. I was not even touching ground when I popped out of the water. I had no chance of winning Round 2 with that beast. I would be buried in the bottom of that smelly canal, jammed into a dug-out gator hole waiting to be tenderized meat. We fought the Grim Reaper that day.

I can't tell you how many people ask me *What were you thinking?* It's my Nip and if she goes, I go. Simple as that. I've received many letters about it, and many would say, 'I never liked you as a golfer and thought you were an idiot, but any man who is willing to die for his dog deserves immense respect.' I love getting those. It does show that we often judge people way too soon. We were very lucky that day. You can't tell me I don't have the best guardian angels in the universe.

Sadly, Nip couldn't dodge the bullet with me in our RV accident that would take Jeannie, Billy and my leg, as she died that day along the side of Route 26 on June 8, 2009.

To this day I still call my newer German Shepherd Munch, "Nip" at times, a decade later.

Munch was given to me by a pro-am partner I played with way back in 1990 or so. I had not seen or talked to him since then and received a call telling me who he was and he said that he had two German Shepherd's and those dogs' breeder was having some new pups. He mentioned that he plays in the pro-ams every year in Dallas but his best day on the course was with me, so he wanted to gift me another pup for losing my baby.

At first I didn't think I would be ready since I was still unable to walk let alone take care of a new dog, and said thanks but not now. A few days went by and something just kept telling me that I needed to get this pup. I called him back and told him that if the offer was still on the table, I would do it. Four months had passed since the accident that had killed Nip so I flew out to Dallas to see Bob and meet my new pup. I had asked my friends on my blog for names and they had some great ones but I hadn't decided yet.

The meeting was great and I couldn't thank Bob enough, so as I was driving I started to think about a name and suddenly thought I needed to honor Bob some way for gifting me this cute pup. "Bob" as the name for the animal was out of the question. But his last name was Muncher so I went with "Munch." I thought it was a classic name. A few weeks later I found out I was dead-off on the name. Bob's name was Bob Munger. *Shit, I'm not changing it now.* So if there's a "Bob Munch" out there, my dog is named after you my friend.

I'm a dog person of the first order and have had over 30 dogs in my life. The first two Nips were insanely smart and loyal to me like no other dogs. Munch puts them to shame. If I walked through fire Munch wouldn't hesitate either. He's off-the-charts smart and extremely loyal- he was like this from day one. He just attached himself and never left my side. As I type away his head is on my lap. He too saved me from losing my marbles.

5/

Ray Floyd & Truth

Age: 25
Legs: 2

W e finished playing the second round of the 1997 Masters and shockingly neither Arnold Palmer nor myself shot 63 to make the cut. Regardless, the media was all around us as we finished. The press always wanted to talk to the King of course, and they loved my Mouth of Mystery, since no one knows what will come out of it. The media were asking a lot of questions so I told them the story about the beer with Arnie and why I did it. My thinking then, as it is today, was simple—tell the truth and you can't get in trouble. I mentioned that I've had a wild run of playing with superstars for the first time. I told them Jack Nicklaus was a classic day, and Seve was a day of confrontation, and Arnie was fun as shit, and Ray Floyd was a dirtball to play with "until he cheated." I mentioned how absolutely blessed I felt to have played with these top-notch players.

They knew about the Seve story but wanted to know what I meant about Floyd. I just said he was a dirtball to play with until he cheated. *What do you mean?* they collectively asked again. I told them the story about years earlier, way back when I was a new nobody on tour, and I was playing the final round in Miami at the Doral resort. My good friend Bob Boyd and I made the cut but we're in last place going into Sunday's final round. Local super-stud Ray Floyd was also going to be in the first group off with us that Sunday. Ray wanted to win Doral badly (he considered it his fifth major) and he's pissed that he's not in contention. The fact that he was playing with two malakas he'd never heard of ensured his mood was dark.

Bob and I were both excited- we made the cut, which we didn't routinely do in those days, and we're playing with Raymond flipping Floyd! When we got to the first tee Ray didn't say one word to us, not one single word. For the next ten holes he said squat, diddly-shit I'm telling you. So we get it. We're scum and he's pissed. So be it.

On the par-5 tenth-hole at Doral Floyd goes for the green in two but hits this pull-hook that never even sniffs getting over a little finger of water 200 yards ahead. Remember, these are persimmon woods and you paid dearly for a bad swing back then. I had pushed my drive and my second shot, so I slapped my third shot up onto the green. Floyd was on the left edge with Bob right in the middle of the fairway. Floyd looks at him and says "Boy, I'm dropping here."

Really? "Boy"? Wow.

Floyd hits it to about fifty feet and is laying four after his drop. Bob turns to me as I'm walking towards him and says in his North Carolina drawl, "Grain! Grain! The goddamn Masters and PGA Champion is cheatin'! Whatrewegonnadooo?"

I look at Bob. "I don't know what we're going to do, we're nobodies," I said. Shaken, Bob gets over his shot and literally push-shanks his wedge dead right. He ends up making double-bogey. Floyd drains his bomb for a par. Silence is king now.

On the next hole Floyd hits his shot to six feet for an easy birdie putt. He proceeds to three-whack and makes a bogey. As we're walking up the incline to the 12th tee, the three of us shoulder to shoulder, Bob says out loud and clearly: "Serves the cocksucker right for cheatin'."

I said nothing but was laughing my ass off inside. Floyd then began talking to us both like we were his long-lost best friends, asking whether we're married or have kids and all the other stuff you typically get out of the way on the first tee. Hence, "He was a dirtball to play with until he cheated."

Now, there's not one bone in my body that believes Ray Floyd is a cheater. He was simply pissed at himself for playing like a pig at his fifth favorite venue. I believe the light went off and he realized he probably didn't take a good drop so he just started to chat us up. We never told any of the organizers or the tour or the officials. Bob told his friends and I told my friends and the story got a lot of mileage because it's a classic story, and that was that until the 1997 Masters.

After I opened my mouth the media then goes to Ray and asks for his response to the story. "You have to consider the source, it's Ken Green," Floyd said.

Then I'm hit with a $3,000 fine for simply telling the story! I went directly to the Commissioner, Tim Finchem, with whom I have a hate-hate relationship. I am fighting this all the way.

In my meeting with Finchem I said, "Hold on here, I have five witnesses that will tell you the exact same story I just told the media and you." I explained that I was not trying to call him out but just telling the truth about how weird things happen when I play with a superstar. Mister Moral Integrity said to me, "The truth doesn't matter."

I said, "If the truth doesn't matter why are we even talking then?" I told him that I felt this was all simply personal against me and also, "You suck." This is the same Commissioner who didn't have the decency to call me after an unexpected death in my family. But he sure knows how to fine me $1,000 for drinking a beer with Arnold Palmer.

When Tim passes on I'm going to write on his tombstone, The Truth Does Matter.

6/

Green Sauce

Age: 32
Year: 1990
Legs: 2
Wife: #2
Location: Miami airport headed to Hong Kong Open

The terminal was hustling and bustling like you would expect in the early evening hours of the international departures lounge at Miami International Airport. Ellen was playing one of her golden oldies—one that had caused trouble for me with other spousal-travel partners in the past: the double-edged and always tricky "I'm-not-sure-the-kids-will-be-alright" gambit. Not unlike Savera years earlier, Ellen, a mere hour before our plane to Hong Kong was to depart, had begun getting cold feet about leaving the kids alone while we were away for the Hong Kong Open.

"I totally understand, but we've done everything we could to make sure they're going to be fine," I said, knowing that she could hear in my voice that I was not about to put up a fight if she wanted to stay. That didn't seem to be what she wanted to hear.

"But Brad has that science assignment and Brooke has her T-ball game that could make the difference between the team making the semifinals or getting turfed from the tournament," she pleaded.

"I understand," I said, wondering if the fact that I was getting paid to fly 5,000 miles to compete in an *actual* professional sporting event for hundreds of thousands of dollars had crossed her mind.

"Listen, I totally hear you. Just stay. I understand," I said, hoping that would be the end of it as the gate agent announced the boarding of Flight 303 to Hong Kong.

"What, you're just going to leave me?" she asked, staring at me a little too long. This was getting serious.

"I don't want to but if you're scared of leaving the kids you're not going to have a good time. And frankly, if you're going to be distracted and brooding about the kids it's going to throw my game off and we'll have made the trip for nothing," I reasoned.

"Fuck you Ken," said Ellen as she stormed off. I nodded and walked to a vending machine to get some candy. I had indeed had this issue rear its ugly head in the past. Ten years earlier, my first wife, Savera, had been unable to soothe the crying Ken Jr. and insisted we stop every hour to tend to his crying. So much so that I missed qualifying for the Miami event that year. But that was when I was 23 and didn't have a pot to piss in; I had no money, only prospects.

Today was quite different. I had already won eight pro golf tournaments, including 5 times on the PGA Tour. I had played in the Ryder Cup the previous year, which in itself highlighted another Ellie (her nickname when she was having an out-of-body meltdown) implosion, and today I was being paid $40,000 just to show up to play the Hong Kong event. And here I was sitting at the gate with my Tupperware container of pasta sauce and no travel partner.

The final boarding call came and I frantically started to scan the terminal for Ellen. She was nowhere to be seen. My pasta bucket stared at me as if to say, *Guess we're headed off to cover some Asian noodles without Ellen.* I shook my head at my fortune as the gate agent was announcing final call for boarding. I could just imagine Ellen being a no-show and my having to send all her bags back from Hong Kong; the expense and time-suck that would entail made me queasy.

I stood up, collected my belongings and walked towards the gate slowly, craning my neck behind me to see if I could catch a glimpse of my wife.

As I approached the gate I saw Ellen, apparently waiting for *me*. She was talking to a gate agent and scowling, which in turn was matched by the scowl of the gate agent, now both looking at me. Seems as though I was now the pampered and spoiled golfer waltzing up to the plane while everyone else waited for his Highness- just your typical professional athlete prima donna. I walked up to my welcoming party and they clucked in unison, stepping aside so I could pass.

"Glad you made it," Ellen said as I walked by her and her new friend.

We took our seats in first-class, a perk provided by the tournament. Ellen took the container of pasta sauce she had made and placed it safely under her seat. The sauce was an Ellen brainchild- the result of my desire to steer clear of unfamiliar Asian spices. If you've ever spent months on-end living out of a suitcase, traveling from hotel to hotel, the one thing you quickly realize is that your diet (and your waistline) will take the brunt of the damage. If you're playing golf across the world in foreign lands and you're trying to win, keeping some type of dietary consistency is crucial.

In my previous forays overseas to Japan and other Asian countries I had realized the one thing in great abundance in those locales was noodles, and while the sauces that accompanied them could be decent, to my admittedly American palate, the distasteful ones outnumbered the tasty ones. As a solution, Ellen had offered to bring a large container of spaghetti sauce with us—whereby we just had to order noodles, and voila, Asian-American spaghetti and sauce. It was a solution that I had endorsed 100%- after all, I was walking six miles each day during the tournament, so the carbs would get used, no question about that.

The flight attendants were offering drinks and putting away coats and the like. I was hoping Ellen would have a drink and we could put this behind us, but she was still hot.

"If anything happens I want you to know you'll be to blame," she said, not even looking at me. That was too much for me to handle. I had bent over backwards for those kids, even going so far as wanting to adopt hers- but their father wouldn't allow it. To be told that I was willfully endangering them was beyond the pale.

"For Christ's sake Ellen, please don't come. Please get off the plane right now and go take care of the kids. I can't do this the entire time. I thought you would calm down after you got on the plane but this is insane. Please, please, get off the plane while you still can."

Ellen looked at me, reached under the seat, grabbed the container of pasta sauce and proceeded to pour it over my head. It wasn't bad. Then we took off and seven days later I won the Hong Kong Open.

7/

World's Worst Gambler

Age: All
Legs: 2
Wife: #2

There are a few things that seem to be common to professional athletes of all types; one of which is gambling. In the eyes of my wife at the time, I was the worst gambler on earth.

As Ellen had done with my brother and sister, I was strongly discouraged from seeing my mother as well. This was the mother who had worked three jobs so that I could pursue my dream of playing pro golf- and now my wife, only after we had married, decided she didn't want me spending time with my mother. She also forbade me from giving my mom any money. And while I may be a moron, I wasn't about to cut off my mother.

So how does a guy squirrel away $50,000 or $60,000 a year without the Evil Eye of Ellen noticing? I devised a simple plan. I told Ellen that every time I went to the casinos I lost money, regardless of whether I did or not. If I lost $2,000 I would write a check to the casino for $5,000 and get $3,000 back, and gave that to my mom. If I happened to win $4,000 I would write another check for $5,000 so I could give her $9,000. Often Mark Calcavecchia, Payne Stewart, Paul Azinger, Freddy Couples, Blaine McCallister, and I would gamble in our practice rounds. I would do the same there but with smaller amounts. We often played for decent amounts but a thousand or so was usually the most you could lose, and I 'lost' every time!

My goal was to give mom $50,000-$60,000 a year so she could do as she wanted without fear of going broke. She was still working one job at this point so it simply helped her along. It was the least I could do for the sacrifices she made for me.

While in the middle of our divorce case Ellen and her lawyer paraded in a big blown-up check I had written to the Mirage Casino in Las Vegas. The check was for $10,000 and it was being used to show the divorce judge that I was an out-of-control gambler. I was used to seeing big, outsized checks and this was three feet by six feet- it was beautiful I tell you, *beautiful.*

So as they sat there telling the judge I was a degenerate gambling mongrel I wanted so badly to tell them where the money was going, but I knew it would just create more problems than me being labeled a terrible person and a problem gambler (I know!). I say things all the time that aren't politically correct or appropriate because I don't really care what people think of me, so it was absolutely in my nature to spill the beans in a situation like this, especially when it would make Ellen look terrible. But I didn't. I didn't because as I say, I may be a moron but I'm not stupid and I knew if I did reveal my little plan I would not be able to give my mother any more money. So instead I sat there and took a beating in the courtroom. So Ellen, if you're reading this, the joke is on you. Sorry, not sorry.

**

One of the strange things of my life, as much as I have been through, as terrible as it might have been at times with depression and pain and life-altering tragedy, the big guy upstairs has always looked out for me it seems. I can't tell you how often I've won money when I was so desperate.

In the late 1990s, when I was flat broke and with Sue, I still had some playing privileges on tour so I would get into a few events here and there. I played in the Bob Hope Classic but didn't get into the event the following week, but I knew I was going to get into the AT&T at Pebble Beach which was the week after that. I decided to stay out on the West Coast and spend my week at the Mirage where I was given a suite by the Wynn family who owned the casino. I had met them through a pro-am a few years earlier and had stayed friendly with them. They had a fantastic facility called Shadow Creek where I was allowed to play and practice the entire week. There are typically only about five groups a day on the course and they treat you like you're the King of Morocco. For the next six days all I did was play golf with my friend Mike Pascal, brother-in-law of Steve Wynn. For the entire week I won $800 on the golf course. I never once placed a bet in a casino for the whole week, not one. The last night there I said *Screw it, I'm going to take the $800 free money and see what happens.* Five hours later I had $105,000 in my briefcase, crazy-glued to my hands. That money kept us afloat the rest of the year.

There was another time when I was basically stuck in Connecticut because Ellen of Troy had issued an arrest warrant for me. She did this every time I was late with the $13,500 monthly alimony. She did it not because she cared about the money but to keep me from seeing my son, Hunter.

At this point I was making zero on tour and was two months ($27,000) in the hole with alimony. I couldn't travel to Florida to see Hunter because the second I stepped foot in the State I would be arrested for defaulting on alimony. So I took the $1,000 I had in the bank and went to Foxwoods Casino about an hour away. Two hours later I counted my chips and had exactly $27,000 in front of me. I cashed them in, went straight to the bank and wired the money to my lawyer. The next day I jumped on a plane to Florida to see my son.

In early 2000 Calc and I were at Foxwoods- he was in town for the Greater Hartford Open and I was in Connecticut for the summer. He called me up and said to meet him at the casino. We often just split our winnings or losses because that's what friends do. This time we were both on fire but I cooled off and told him to just run with the wolves while I sat and watched. A few hours and a dozen beers later he had $110,000 in hand and we decided that was enough.

I can honestly tell you that it felt like I was being helped by powers beyond my control. I won't bore you with other similar adventures except to tell you that in the whole decade of the 2000's, when I needed money, the casinos were great to me. I won $50,000 two other times and more than $20,000 three other times. I'm not saying I can't lose because when I did have money I often did just that. I'm simply saying I've won a lot of money when I needed it the most. To this day

I very seldom go to the casinos because I don't want to get greedy and press my luck- who knows, I may need the desperation jackpot one more time.

One time when I was doing well on tour I had lost my gambling quota for the trip and was just hanging out in my hotel room. For some reason I was prompted to look under the bed, and what did I find up against the wall but three chips that literally had dust on them. Two were for $1,000 and one for $500. I thought it was an omen from the skies. I went straight down to try my luck with my newfound money. I was back in my room empty-handed 20 minutes later. Sometimes skies lie.

8/

Not So Fast Mr. Reaper

There are many who think strange occurrences are just that. Others say it's The Big Guy Upstairs. I truly believe we're on this planet to learn, so damn it I'm trying hard now. I'm just not very bright. I'm sure we've all had close calls with death (or maybe not) and whether you believe your salvation was intentional or not, I choose to believe I'm here not because of dumb-ass luck but because of dumb-ass luck and some help from our friends on the other side. Since I don't believe in spouting my beliefs about the after-life and The Man Upstairs, I'll just document a few times I should have died and didn't, and you can decide whether it's pure luck, or whether I had a little help.

The three insanely close calls to death I had in Honduras came about before I realized how bad my father's drinking problem was and how it affected his ability to drive a car. I was 11. He would blow, full-speed, through stop signs and stop lights on a regular basis. One time we missed a bus by a matter of inches. Another time we were driving up a precipitous, curving mountain road when I looked out the window and saw nothing but the bottom of a cliff a thousand yards below, with my father driving with one eye covered. To this day I am amazed we didn't go over the cliff- I can still visualize the drop.

When I was 17 my friend Kirk and I drove down to Florida for a week of golf. I was so scared Kirk would fall asleep while driving that I never really fell asleep as the passenger. So when he got tired and we switched I of course fell asleep doing 60mph. We went off I-95 at full speed and stuck the car in mud. We somehow managed to get the car back through the mud and onto the highway. When we did we saw a big lake just to the right of us. If I had waited another couple of seconds to fall asleep and go off the road, we probably would have been killed.

Once my career got into full gear there was obviously a lot of driving. I preferred driving since I took my dogs with me when I could. Most tournaments are scheduled geographically close to each other so they're typically within a day's drive. If I made the cut I would leave Sunday for the next city, packing up my stuff and hitting the road in order to get there for the obligatory pro-ams and other glad-handing that are part of my job as a PGA Tour pro. I would relish these opportunities to play with fans and corporate execs, and it was because of my belief that our fans and sponsors were the ones paying our salaries that I threw caution to the wind and hit the road when I probably should have slept over and left early the next morning. Three times I went off the highway at full speed without ever damaging the car or myself. Every time I went off the road it was into an empty field as opposed to one filled with trees. That luck would hold until June 8, 2009.

Up to that point those were really the good old days of traveling. You know, the days when you had to use what we once called "maps." One time I was driving from Ohio to Kingsmill in Virginia for the next PGA Tour event. Being the brainiac that I am I took a peek at the map to see if there might be a quicker way to get from northern Pennsylvania to southern Pennsylvania. I located what looked like a decent road with a handy shortcut, and off I went. The road was only a two-laner but I was making good time. Going about 60mph I went up a slope and when I got to the top the road suddenly veered dead left. I, naturally, went airborne, flying off the road and down an embankment where I wiped out the Gross Domestic Product of Iowa, in corn.

You can imagine my heart was in full-pump mode. I can't see squat, sitting in this car surrounded by dead corn husks, so I decide to get on top of the roof to formulate a solution to my predicament. I noticed I had wiped out quite a stretch of corn, and in the distance I see a house with a light, which I assumed was the farmer's house. I got back into the car and slowly turned my Olds 98 toward the road and floored it. I made it all the way back to the road. I got out to look at my masterpiece of destruction and it was quite impressive. I knew I should go tell the farmer but he might've shot my ugly ass.

I arrived safely and checked into my room without further incident. The next day I went to the course and when I climbed out of the car I noticed that I had corn-on-the-cob stuck all over the wheels and both bumpers. This would continue to be a theme...

The Innisbrook Copperhead course where they now play the Valspar event used to host the JC Penny mixed-team event. Avid followers of golf know how hard that course is for today's players, so imagine how hard it was for us back then.

For that event one year I played with Barb Bunkowsky, who was also from West Palm Beach so it was a no brainer to pair us up together. That, plus she was a little whacky in the head, like me, so it was a perfect marriage. The course usually humbled us pretty well but one year we had our best finish, which I think was fourth. Once we completed our day we had no choice but to have a congratstail with a couple friends who were watching us, along with Barb's and my good friend Eric "no car" Larson.

The service at the bar was pretty much like today's PGA tour players, slower than snail poop. A mere five hours later we decided we had had enough of this horrible service and decided to head back to West Palm, a three-hour drive.

On standing up we realized that our Barb had either had a few more drinks than we did, or she had the same amount but was much smaller than we were (which was the case). It was then decided I would drive my car and Eric would drive her car. The road back was a two-lane road most of the way with canals and farms all over the place. We decided we were going to be 'smart' and drive cautiously (*yes, I know!*). This meant we were only going about 85mph most of the way (*yes, yes, I know!*). We were cruising along nicely when I crest a hill and sitting in the middle of the road is a dog, from out of nowhere. My instincts took over and I immediately jerked the car to the left. The car stopped spinning after about five or six of them and my heart was now in my head. *Holy shit I'm alive and the dog is too!* Once again that dog was in the perfect spot because twenty yards further down the road and I'm dead in the canal. Suddenly E pulls up, rolls down his window and says, "Stop fucking around G, let's go!" Of course, we made it home safely.

The next morning at seven Ellen wakes me up yelling at me. *What the hell did I do now?* She drags my ass out of bed to the car. She proceeds to show me that each tire has a band of grass wrapped all around the rims. The fenders were full of grass too. "Damn it, Ellen," I said, "We had to attend the after-party for the tour and it was a hula festival. We decorated the car. I'm going back to bed." She didn't buy it but it was the end of that.

So did I have just pure dumb-ass luck or did I have some aid from the powers above? I suppose you will have to decide that on your own. I know I had help; it just wasn't my time to move on.

9/

The Ryder Cup and Stuff

Both the Ryder Cup and The Presidents Cup have reached a point of media insanity, coupled with the players over-thinking the entire process. My biggest complaint with the media coverage is that they make it sound like if you're a rookie you shouldn't be able to play well. These morons seem to forget that either sides' rookies are top-shelf players. They're not some club champ you pulled out of the crowd and said, "Go tee it up for the USA young man."

Then they will go over and over each match like a surgeon conducting an amputation. Look, it's golf. Those who make the most putts, win. Both events are already huge—they don't need any bullshit hype from the media's mental midgets.

Then they will pound you on why you thought the captain did this or that. Once again they over-analyze just so we can hear them speak. No wonder they get over-inflated views of how important they are to golf. I mean, do you think when they're making love to their wives or mistresses they stop the video to discuss the proper techniques for the current position? Enough! Cut your words down by sixty percent and let the golf do the talking. They also make the captains' decisions seem like the be-all-and-end-all of decision making. Let me explain...

In 2014, Phil Mickelson and others on that team threw the bus on top of Tom Watson, their captain. Those 12 dopes got their asses

Then you do it in front of the world? The concept that pairing this pro with that pro is going to win or lose a match is complete bullshit. These are the best players in the world and if they can't get focused and play with anyone from their country, for their country, they're fools. And if you stink up the course, the captain is not to blame. Like everything in life however, there is one exception: It is probably not a good idea to pair a player whose wife may have slept with Dustin Johnson, with Dustin Johnson. That might be tricky, just sayin'.

In my opinion there is really only one decision made by the captain that is important: course set-up prior to starting the event. The home host can do as he sees fit in setting up the course. Here's what The Greatest Captain of All Time would do if he were captain:

I would first find out each players' tendencies to miss off the tee. If I noticed a pattern, for instance, of most of my guys missing left, then I would make sure the rough on the left side, at their approximate driving distance, was not as bad as the other side. I would do the same for their irons and place pins on the greens that favored their misses. The players failed Davis Love at Medinah, blowing that huge lead, but if Love had used his head and used easier pin placements it would've made it much harder for the Euros to win so many matches. It's far harder to make birdies all day long with difficult locations- we lost so many holes with pars. I would also find out the other side's tendencies to see if we could use that to our advantage as well. For instance, in 2018 the American squad was filled with long but crooked drivers. The Euro's captain, Thomas Bjorn, ordered the fairways be narrowed and rough grown to negate any American advantage.

I then ask each player their favorite pin position and other things that I then use to determine how I set up the course.

I would tell the powers that be that only four of my players are attending those stupid dinners each night. There are two or three of them that week alone! In the old days maybe they needed to three of them that week alone! In the old days maybe they needed to attend, but not now.

I'm totally against the new think-tank concept of how to fix our losing Ryder Cup efforts. If we were losing the Presidents Cup as well I might say *Hey, we have to figure things out.* But we're not. The rotten Ryder Cup play is all in their heads. They also need to relax. Those who relax hole everything, those who don't, moan about it. The biggest misconception is the dreaded captain's picks. Europe needs them because some of their guys are playing overseas and others are playing in the U.S. We don't have that issue. The points are not being allocated correctly (the top eight point-getters on the money list are automatically on the team, and the captain gets to choose four additional players—any players he wants). There should be way more points for winning events than finishing a nauseating fifth. The Cups are as equally pressure-filled as trying to win on tour on Sundays. So do we want a guy who top-10s it all the time, or a guy who knows how to win? Keep stacking the deck with fifth-place finishers and what are you gonna get? Whipped, that's what.

The idea that most captains' picks are either guys they know well or are veterans who can help with 'chemistry,' is bull. You might be a veteran who has been fantastic in the past but we all hit a time where we're not what we used to be. The idea that Bubba Watson was not on the 2016 Ryder Cup team was a disgrace to golf. I am not a Bubba fan; he's a whiny cry-baby who blames everyone else for his mental and physical lapses, but he should've been on that team. Two wins that year and he didn't make the team? The same for the European side. Russell Knox won twice on the PGA Tour that year but captain Darren Clarke went with his friend Lee "Yippee" Westwood. Lee has been a great player but he was a total liability. I say let your play be the proof. Just go with the top 12 Americans on the list, period. The new twist is the deadline for earning points to qualify. They don't continue them through the FedEx Cup playoffs. Call me stupid, but why on earth do the last three events (the events that are closest to the actual Cup and most indicative of how you're playing) count so little? It's not like we can't get the team outfits together or the guys who make it at the end can't flip their schedules: "Ahh, gee, gosh, I was going fishing with my father-in-law so I can't make the Ryder Cup, sorry."

It's clear I'm not the sharpest magnet in the game but some of these problems are so easy to fix it's laughable. The PGA of America refuses to make changes, either due to ego or stupidity—I'm honestly not sure which. Tell me you wouldn't be tuned into the tube if they chose the pairings like the Presidents Cup does, "You pick, then I pick." The Ryder Cup just throws a list up versus the list they threw up. No drama, no intrigue.

I would even make a change to how the Presidents Cup does it. I say the host team goes first each time in choosing the two-man team matches. Then the underdog guest gets to pick what team goes up against the other team. For the singles you alternate because who doesn't want to see their best against our best. The next change I would make is again what the Presidents Cup used to do. There should be five matches each session instead of four. The idea that you bust your balls all year to make the Ryder Cup only to sit around picking your nose or scratching your ass when it comes time to actually compete, is sinful. There have been times where you make the team only to watch the captain sit you down and play his veteran/buddy.

I would also rent two houses very close to each other where all the players would stay. If you really want comradery and guys having a blast, that's the way. I might even suggest spending a million to build a house-dorm with great bedrooms and communal spaces where all 12 guys would stay. (Brilliance sneaks up on me, don't you think?)

The PGA Tour and the PGA of America, along with the rest of the powers that be, have made the decision to allow way too many fans into the venue each day. This brings a rowdy, drunken, and impossibly large crowd. I feel for the fans who show up each day to a Ryder or Presidents Cup because they really only see a small amount of actual golf, standing 20 deep in the huge gallery. Why don't we think of the fans for once? I know golf does so much for charity, but why not do more for the fan, too? They have done this for money and money only, and in my opinion it's a disgrace. The $20 million they profit from each event must not be enough.

If you need more proof that money talks and character walks, let's examine the golf courses these events seem to choose in the U.S. In this case, The PGA of America might be bigger whores than the PGA Tour when it comes to picking sites. Why do they keep going back to Whistling Straits so much? Probably because Herb Kohler paid them bazillions of dollars. Does it not blow anyone's mind that the most honest professional sport is being controlled by the greediest

PGA European Tour. No matter where you play these events they will be sell-outs. While tour events are locked in to cities, the Cups and the U.S. Open can be held anywhere and are guaranteed sell-outs.

Nebraska, Kansas, Arkansas, New Mexico, the Dakotas, Tennessee and a couple others are getting belly-bunked. My sources tell me the players do not like Whistling Straits but they've played two PGAs with a Ryder Cup soon coming, because of money. Kiawah is another track that's not liked but they're going back there for another Ryder Cup and a PGA. Either Cup would be more exciting if they were played at my public course, Richter Park, in Danbury, Connecticut.

If any of these organizations did good things with the enormous amount of cash they made I might swallow my words. To date they have failed miserably in growing the game I have loved and the game that probably saved my life. We have 50 States, so get off your greedy asses and figure out a way to bring some events to these underserved States, damn it.

The most exciting course for a cup event might very well be the TPC Stadium Course. Tell me you wouldn't get stoked about watching an event there.

Don't misunderstand these complaints because I love the Cup events. I've been fortunate enough to represent two countries in three events in my lifetime. The first was in Honduras. As a pre-teen I once represented Honduras in the Junior Central American Championships. How they loved my Spanish. They let me play because I was the best young golfer back then and they needed me to fill out the team. I was given temporary citizenship. The event was held in Managua, Nicaragua, and I don't recall how we did but it was fun for sure.

The Ryder Cup I was fortunate to play in was at The Belfry in England in 1989. The USA had lost in '87 so the Euros had a 1/2 point edge to start the tournament. That practice needs to end and end soon. The idea that the new team pays a price for the previous team is downright idiotic and I honestly can't believe the players haven't stepped up and said, "Enough." Did Jack or Tiger ever have to give everybody else in the field a shot advantage because they won the U.S. Open the year before? Either you call it a tie or you have a playoff.

I couldn't wait to get to the UK because Calc had told me how much fun the Ryder Cup was and I was being given the chance to honor and serve my country, which I'm very proud of. Even when we do make mistakes we're still the greatest country that has ever existed, in my humble opinion.

Back then we didn't have 23 vice-captains, 12 drink-holders, 6 service-girls and all the other insane things they do today. Ray Floyd was my captain and we had no vice-captains. I was really concerned about how often Floyd would play me because as you know I wasn't exactly tight with him or the other players, save for Calc. The truth is they didn't know me nor I them. The one thing I had going for me was Calc, who had won the British Open that year and I had won that year myself, so that was at least good. I was known as a go-for-broke guy like Calc. Not too bright, also like Calc. I had a whacked-out wife, so did Calc. We were obviously a pretty dynamic duo- like spray cheese on saltines.

Representing the USA was an incredible honor and an absolute blast, but as great as it was, I still had to keep something secret from everyone or Floyd might never have played me: I had a complete mess back home.

I had arranged to have a family member watch our three kids back in the U.S. during the week of the Ryder Cup. Unbeknownst to me this family member really wanted to use the week as a vacation of fun and games instead of actually watching the kids. By the time Thursday came along I had handled the mess as best I could but Ellen was going nuts. "What the fuck is the matter with your family?!" she screamed. "You're a terrible judge of character! I'm going home!"

"Ellen you can't go home," I replied. "I know it's not right that she's going out all night and having other friends actually do the babysitting, but the kids are still okay. I've made other arrangements. If you leave under the guise of some "family emergency" then I'm not going to get played, period." Man, did I plead.

Ellen said she didn't give a fuck about the stupid Ryder Cup or me sitting. "I'm leaving," she said.

"Ellen, I'm supposed to play the first match in the morning. There's no way in hell you can do this," I tried reasoning with her. This went on all night long. I got zero sleep.

Despite the flaming diaper-fire that was my home life, Calc and I steamrolled our alternate-shot match. At this particular format (two players on the same team alternating each shot) Calc and I were a great duo because neither of us gave a flying fart whether we left the other with an awkward shot. We are both aggressive players and when you play aggressively you will often leave yourself in a predicament for the next shot, so we were both used to hitting difficult shots. We were also both firm putters of the ball so we were used to three and four footers coming back for par. We were a perfect marriage, unlike the one I was actually in.

We were on No. 14 and way up in our match when Captain Floyd came up to me and asked me how I felt and was I ready to go again? I didn't want to assume anything, so I simply said, "Ray, I'm putting the eyes out of the ball today so if you're going to play me twice, now is the time."

I mean, when one of the best putters on earth at the time, after winning his previous match handily, says he's putting lights out and he wants in, you would think that it would be a no-brainer to play him again. But Floyd elected to sit me, and Calc lost his next match. We'll never know for sure but there's no doubt in my mind Calc and I would've won that match. I elected to watch the Calc match because I knew going back to the room only meant a full-blown scream-fest with Ellen.

We were having a team meeting that night where we all talked about X, Y or G. When I got up I spoke from where I always speak: my heart. I told the team that I was honored to be there and that I wanted to thank all of the guys for treating me like I was a friend.

"I didn't know many of you to start with but you're not so bad after all," I joked. Lanny Wadkins then chirped in saying, "Shit Green, we were all petrified of your ass, but you're not so bad yourself." A great laugh we all had after that one. I will always remember the team get-together that night.

Friday night was another Ellen beat down on me, complete with yell-fest. The good news was that I managed to talk Ellen out of leaving. After watching the matches she finally realized how important and tense the Ryder Cup was. So at the very least I knew she wasn't leaving and boning me and our team and country.

The next day Calc and I did what we do best: steamroll through the alternate shot match. Alternate shot was much harder back then than it is now. People have forgotten how much the equipment of that era was so inferior to today. Granted we were all using the same equipment so to us it was simply golf.

Back then you paid dearly for a bad swing, but what is lost on many is the price paid back then when you hit a mediocre golf shot.

Today a mediocre 5-iron leaves you a 20-30 footer. Back then, if you missed with a 5-iron you missed the green, or if you were lucky, you were left with a 60-footer.

The second alternate shot match against Ronan Rafferty and Christy O'Connor Jr. went even smoother than our first one. We were just both hitting and going. I have no idea if our style confused our opponents or maybe it was the fact that we just never worried about our mishit shots. In alternate shot you can't worry about what you're doing to your partner, period. And neither of us cared if we left our partner with a tough shot—we both knew what we were there to do. We also didn't jump up and down and get excited after each hole like they seem to do now. Just because you win a hole doesn't mean you go into a frenzy. It's hard to play golf if you're going up and down with emotions. I firmly believe the key to playing your best golf is just making sure you're the same person on the course as you are off the course. If you're a talker (Lee Trevino, Ken Green, Phil Mickelson) then you should just gab your ass off, and vice versa. The powers to be in golf want each golfer to be a certain way. "Be who you are or you will never peak," is my view. Arnold Palmer could never be Jack Nicklaus. Ken Green could never be Nick Faldo, thank the lord, (he's a complete jackass then and still is today). Calc and I were just being us- two stupid, fat-ass, gambling, go-for-broke nut-jobs.

Floyd had the two of us go again for the best ball matches. We played against their two best Spaniards, Seve Ballesteros and his protégé Jose Maria Olazabal. They were a great Ryder Cup duo. Calc and I did what we always do, just go hit it. In this particular instance however, we ran into a buzz-saw Spaniard with one hot-ass putter. Jose made four 30-footers in the first five holes! Ouch. We never had a chance after that. Neither one of us played well, and that happens. On the sixth hole both Calc and Seve were out of the hole. Jose and I both had about 16 feet for birdie. I rolled mine over the edge and it stopped about a foot or so past the hole where he gave it to me. Jose hit his putt about two feet from the hole and didn't wait for me to give it to him (only your opponent can 'give' you a putt) and just picked it up. The next hole was a par-3 so we had a bit of a wait, so I approached Jose.

"Jose listen, do me a favor and don't pick up a ball unless we actually give it to you, okay?" I said as non-threatening as I could muster. Before Jose could reply Seve walked up and started rambling on about Mark McCumber having done something similar to them the previous day. Now I'm thinking, *Oh boy, I'm going to have Round Two with Seve after our little run-in that year at Augusta.*

Now, I've been sleeping only a couple hours a night due to my cage-matches with Ellen, I'm stressed out, and I'm playing the most important international golf tournament in history. So I'm ready to go off on Seve for trying to turn this around and blaming us for the error. Legally, within the rules of golf, I could have called a penalty and we would have been given the hole. It recently happened in a Cup event (the Solheim Cup), and Seve himself would have done exactly that. But before I could go off on Seve, Jose stepped in and said, "No Seve, he's right, I did pick it up without hearing anything from them." I respect Jose tremendously for diffusing a situation that was escalating quickly. Seve was a great golfer but as a person on the golf course he was a complete ass. He played mind games with everyone, he would move, he might cough here and there. It's sad because that man had such talent and charisma. Sadly he died at age 53 from a brain tumor.

We were neck and neck with the Euros going into the final singles matches. Floyd asked me where I wanted to start. I said I wanted to go first because I'm as fast a player as there is and I don't feel like waiting on these slow moving ducks out there. Floyd put me eighth. So much for first. *Then why ask?*

This time I was going up against another Spaniard, Jose Maria Canizares. He was very nice to play with so it was obvious he didn't get the Seve gene. I played really well- I was the most under par except for Tom Kite who went crazy and birdied like seven out of 11 and wiped out his opponent.

Canizares also played well with the exception of a couple of doubles. He got lucky on 17 and made birdie by draining a 15-footer with the help of a bounce to the left and into the hole. I had two putted for birdie so we were tied going into the last hole. The 18th at The Belfry had given many of the Americans trouble off the tee where they kept driving it into the water trying to clear it. Fortunately for me I didn't have the distance to carry the water, which if you were able to do would allow your second shot to be 40 yards closer. We both hit good tee shots but Canizares was away.

Though it has now been redesigned, the final green at The Belfry was a severely sloped three-tier green. The first tier was an insanely tough four-foot slope. The pin was just over the edge of the first tier. Jose hit first. He proceeded to pull-hook a 2-iron. Just to the left of the green was a greenside bunker and then nothing but water after that. There was no doubt in my mind Jose was going to miss the bunker and go into the water. I was half right. He missed the sand but flew it into the grass lip on the water-side of the bunker, where it must have hit a stone or rock because the ball bounced dead right and up and over the bunker onto the back of the green. I could not believe it! I was stunned and annoyed that such a terrible shot was magically rewarded by ending up on the green, but luck is part of the game- I had to keep going.

I had 209 yards to the top of the ridge on the first tier of the green, and 212 yards to the hole. I choose to hit my cleek, which to the non-initiated is a cross between a wood and a hybrid, before we had ever heard of the term "hybrid" and when "wood" actually meant "wood." I proceeded to hit one of my top-five under-the-gun shots I've ever hit. The ball went higher and softer than even I knew how to hit it back then, plus it was straight at the pin. Tom Kite was there and before it landed he said, "Great pressure shot!" We watched as the ball flew 209 yards. We figured it would hit soft and trundle up to within a few feet of the hole. We figured wrong. To this day I have no idea how or why what happened, happened.

Instead of releasing forward on landing, as low-loft shots are supposed to do, the ball somehow went backwards and then rolled down the slope to a nice 90-foot putt going up Mount FUKenGreen. My 209-yard shot ended up being 170 yards.

Now I'm stuck with an impossible putt where if you don't hit the first putt hard enough you're looking at another 90-footer. I hit a good putt but it rolled about 15 feet past the hole. Jose rolled his 3rd shot down to tap-in range. I then hit a perfect putt but had the wrong read and missed the putt left-edge. I had lost my singles match. We then won the last few matches but the Euros had won 14 points, which meant they kept the Cup due to the idiotic tie-goes-to-the previous-winner rule.

To this day I refuse to say we lost. A tie is a tie. The last match was Curtis Strange vs. Ian Woosnam. On 18 I watched Curtis hit a 2-iron 18 inches short of where my ball hit into the slope, which should have killed its momentum, but it didn't – it actually popped up and over the ridge and to a couple feet for a tap in. If you believe in the Big Guy (or Big Gal) and believe that some things are meant to be, that hole is the perfect example: Earlier, Jose's ball should have, at best, been in the bunker, and mine should have never gone backwards.

But against all odds, they did. And despite the fact that I lived and died by the sword of kismet, I was devastated- the way I lost was so hard for me to handle. Then the idea that I cost the team and the USA the Ryder Cup was just devastating. I stole someone's sunglasses so people wouldn't see my eyes filled with tears during the closing ceremonies.

When I got back to the room Ellen decided to go off on me again. Just another day in the life of Kenny Green, I thought. *I will try again tomorrow*, was the only thing that ran through my head. We attended the dinner and awards ceremony and then went back to the room where I was going to meet the team and two of my best friends who had flown over to watch the Ryder cup: Greg Begler, aka Bags, and Don Watkins, aka Wad. Once we got to the room Ellen got on the phone and more trouble ensued because we couldn't reach anyone at home so she assumed the worst. Then things went ballistic so I had to bail on meeting my friends and the other players. I was really aggravated because it turns out that my friends met up with some of the other players and started playing whiffle ball in the hotel hallways. I was MVP in whiffle ball four years in a row, damn it.

I will always cherish the Ryder Cup even though it was tainted for me. My marriage pretty much ended there but wouldn't fail for another year or so.

I also represented the USA in the Asahi Cup. It was the start of what is now the Presidents Cup. Then, they divided the world into four parts: America, Europe, Asia and the rest of the world. Even Iceland could get in, but no one qualified.

We played in Japan and all the big names showed up. I have a few distinct memories from the Asahi cup. We won, so that was a bonus. It was a medal match-play event where you kept your score against your opponent's score. We did a pre-qualifier and then the two teams went into the last day's playoff. So in reality you had to play really good golf to win. Ronan Rafferty was Europe's Order of Merit for a few years in a row and I ended up playing him one day. I shot a good 68 but lost to his better 66. We won the day so I was fine with my loss. That night I just happened to stop the elevator from closing and who but the mighty Greg Norman is in there with a lady on his arm. He asked how I did so I told him I lost to Rafferty 66-68. He then asks how the hell I could lose to that moron. I looked at him and said, "It's easy Greg, I didn't have a local lovely keeping me warm at night like you do."

10/

Wins

1985 Buick Open

They say your first win is a special one and I believe that to some degree. That's why I made a chapter out of it in this book, but in case you skipped that chapter, I wanted to make sure you didn't miss my first win. After all, I don't have that many.

I can't say I had any inkling that the 1985 Buick Open was going to be my week. I had no clue I was going to play well that week much less end up with the title. All I know is that for whatever reason, once I got near the lead, I was only thinking *All you have to do is have the best score at the end damn it.* There is nothing to be nervous about until it's over. Even though I don't know how or why, that's how I've always felt and it served me very well that week and the others to follow. If you are thinking about anything other than your score during a round you will probably not be the best you can be. In other words, you'll be trunk-slamming before the weekend.

1985 King Hassan Trophy

I was invited to go to Rabat, Morocco, so my sister and caddie Shelley and I decided *why not go play?* Today it's a European event but back then it was a combo of European players and about 30 American players. The underrated great Billy Casper was like The Godfather to us young nuts. He was without a doubt the nicest of the big studs of that era in that he loved talking to you and helping you in any way he could. It was an honor to get to know him. The media was so stuck up on the big three they forgot how good this man played, and he won fifty-plus times to boot.

We arrived in Marrakesh, which for many was a shock. They were seeing how the poor lived in other countries and how nasty their conditions were. Shelley and I were used to this from Honduras. We then got to play the oldest course in Africa which was unique and quite the goofy little layout.

The Prince then entertained us at a special luncheon where I was able to try the most god-awful food on earth. No wonder they're all skinny over there. Bruce Fleisher told me it would be an insult not to try their special desserts, so I tried the pie. It was Pigeon Pie but the gullible me was told it was only a name and there were no actual pigeons in it. I took one bite and hit thirty tiny pigeon bones. I choked on it while they laughed. I got the last laugh however since I won the tournament.

I was tied with Andrew Magee but made birdie on the last hole to pick off my second win of the year. I was given a dagger as the trophy and it's still my favorite trophy I've ever won. Bob Murphy had his appraised at thirty-thousand dollars, so it was nice to know all the diamonds, rubies and emeralds were legit. During the divorce we had it appraised and it came back at only $8,000. The jeweler boned me, damn it. I never said anything to them because I feared for the jeweler's life. If the new King, who was the Prince I had met, found out the jeweler was valuing their biggest golf trophy at a measly 8k they would probably have him killed for dishonoring the Kingdom. Regardless of the appraised value, it's priceless to me.

1986 International

As August of 1986 rolled around, I was having just a so-so year. Some say the hardest thing to do is win your second PGA Tour event. I'm not sure about that because you could really just keep saying that about each next win. The International was a brand-new tourney, with a new format. We were going to play Stableford points—and it was a survive or die system. That meant you either moved on to the next day or you went home. The first day, 78 guys teed off and half made it through. The next day the other 78 did the same. So now we're at the final 78 where the top 24 points from that day move on to Saturday. On Saturday the top 12 make it to Sunday for the final round. Greg Norman and a few other stars who didn't make it to Sunday started to complain, because that's what we pro golfers do best. Deflecting is easier than blaming ourselves. In reality though, once Sunday arrives, there are only about ten guys or so who could win a regular (medal play) tour event too, so why bitch?

I managed to get through the first day fairly easily but the second day was tough conditions, but I made it to the third day. I had a pretty good day on Saturday and made it through to Sunday. Not one of us knew what we had to shoot to win the tournament. I just figured, *be the lowest number, dopey.*

The last day was difficult. It was the ultimate pressure cooker, which meant controlling the distance the ball travels might be tricky. We were playing in high-altitude Denver for the first time, so those who couldn't control their adrenaline were doubly in trouble (altitude + adrenaline = who knows where it's going!).

I was four under after 14 which meant 8 points. At this point it was down to about four or five of us. I'll never forget the cameras were walking with me on 14 and one of the reporters said something about all the studs who were complaining about the format. I remember saying into the camera, walking down the fairway, "Well, if they didn't like the format why did they show up? Simple as that."

I got bone-porked on 15 with my birdie putt and was not pleased, if you get my drift. I need at least two birdies to win, with Sindelar and Langer sitting above me. I was thinking 17 was a must-birdie (but easy) par-5. Sixteen and 18 are tough holes. I knew the pins on both holes were far left and because I played a fade I knew I would have to start the ball left of the target with almost zero room for error. I would have to take on one of those tough pins. I thought 18 would be the easier pin to go at but then I thought, *Do you really want to make 18 a do-or-die hole, with all that pressure?* Conversely, if I go at 16 and mess it up I still have a potential eagle at 17. So I decided to go at the false front far left pin on 16. To this day it's still in my top five shots. A perfect 6-iron that started right at the pin and dropped to about 13 feet. I made the putt and went to 17 with full confidence. I birdied 17 and then played 18 safely and pulled off win number two. I didn't realize it but it meant more to me than I thought. It kind of proved to me that my first official win wasn't a fluke and that I did belong out there. So maybe that second win *is* more of a big deal, especially shooting 66 to do it.

1987 Spalding

This was not technically a tour event but was played the first week before the tour started up in January, so many touring pros played in it, with a mix of LPGA stars and some other pros. We played at Pebble Beach and Carmel Valley Ranch.

It was three days of playing with amateurs and then one day with pros. It was great because I was able to bring my brother Billy and friend Eric Larson. I was able to watch those two dopes get hammered every night and have a drunken blast. I couldn't have been happier though because there's nothing better than enjoying your family and friends while you're playing golf.

After three days I'm in the last group with LPGA star Jan Stephenson. It was as tight as it can get but I had a one-shot lead with one to go over the beauty queen. I hit a pathetic shot into the green and left myself a 50-footer. I left it short so had a six-footer for the win. I still remember making a pure stroke on that putt and in it went for the win. I remember Jan trying to hit on me during the last round, trying to shatter my focus. It was a brilliant Seve Ballesteros-like gamesmanship move and might have worked if my brain worked like a normal person's. I mean, she is one great golfer and one beautiful lady.

1988 Canadian Open

It was early September and the year had been a very good and consistent one to date. However, it lacked a win. I had lost two playoffs earlier in the year to Sandy Lyle and Seve Ballesteros.

The Canadian Open that year was at Glen Abbey, which is a Nicklaus course design. It was a typical Jack course in that it was fair off the tee with difficult green complexes. It was, back then, a very long course.

I was in the last group on Sunday. Things were going absolutely perfectly through 11 holes and I had opened up a lead of four shots.

I was hitting on all cylinders. Shot-making was good, the putting was good—it's rare to have both going well. Then *boom*, a storm comes in out of nowhere and they have to postpone the tournament until Monday. I was bummed because I knew it was in the bag, but I figured it could wait.

The next day winter arrived; it was howling and cold as hell. I hate cold weather- once a wuss always a wuss. It was a rough seven holes and my game was on life-support all of a sudden. It seemed like I was bogey-birdie-bogey until I stepped up on 18 with a one-shot lead.

The last hole is a par 5, which back then was reachable in two with a 3-wood if you hit a good shot. Tiger Woods hit one of his famous shots from the fairway bunker with a 6-iron to 15 feet on his way to winning one year.

After a perfect drive I had a 3-wood in my hand, assuming Scott Verplank would make birdie and tie me. I'd be lying if I told you I had full confidence that I was going to pull this shot off, as it had been a seven hole hit-or-miss festival so far. I kept recalling the driver I hit off the fairway to the same green the day before and had stuck it 30 feet from the pin. That was also one of my top five shots of all time because while it was a driver, I managed to hit it with enough spin that it hit the narrow green and stopped.

I waited for what seemed like a day and finally Scott missed his birdie putt. I quickly put away the wood and pulled out a nine-iron and then hit a sand-wedge to fifteen feet and won for the fourth time, and first of the year.

Each year after you win any tournament you are often asked to come back the following year, a few months before the next year's event, for Media Day where you basically shoot the shit and play golf with the media guys. We had it all set up but the week before I was to promote the 1989 Canadian Open they called me and said that it was cancelled. I figured stuff happens so that's that until I show up to the tournament a few months later. There, a press guy comes up to me and asks why I had to bail on the Media Day several months ago. I was like, *What the heck are you talking about, they canceled on me!?*

Turns out the Canadian Golf Association told the media I had to bail, and they subsequently replaced me with another pro. They lied to me and they lied to the media. They did all this because they were afraid of what I was going to say in regards to playing the Million-Dollar Challenge in Sun City, South Africa. It was at the height of apartheid and the world thought Sun City should be boycotted. I was so pissed and disappointed, to say the least. I went flying into the head of the CGA and ripped him a new one. I never said anything to the press about it though. The bottom line is that if they had an issue about what I might say they should have told me they had concerns, not lie to everyone about it. It was a classless act, something that surprised me coming from the normally forthright Canadians.

1988 Milwaukee

I had just won in Canada the previous week and this week it's off to Milwaukee for the GMO. So far my track record of playing well after a win was nothing special so who knew which Ken Green would show up.

I started out with two decent rounds but was not on top, or even close. Saturday was a special day where once again ball-striking and my putter were madly in love with each other. Seven birdies and two eagles later I had shot a 61 and was now leading the Greater Milwaukee Open.

Shooting 61 in those days was like 59 today, it's seldom done. It's hard to follow up a great round with another one unless you're Johnny Miller, who seemed to do it in his sleep when he was hot. However, I had the singular goal of winning, so it wasn't hard to focus.

I recall getting off to a good start on Sunday and was on a good pace, even widening the lead. Then on six I started getting really light-headed and wobbly. I fought it off as best I could but I was starting to turn a bunch of shades of white. I teed off on eight and took a few steps and then dropped to the ground. My heart was pounding and I was in and out of it. The paramedics were called, and they did what they could do and recommended I go to the hospital immediately. Not on your life was I leaving. I managed to get up and steady my walk. I was still out of it though because I had a six-footer for par and all I could see were three balls in front of me. It was a bizarre sensation but I had no choice but to putt because I was going to be sent home if I dropped again. I somehow made the putt and by the next hole I was perfectly fine. Thanks to three eagles and many birdies I cruised to my second win in consecutive weeks. It was also the year I led the PGA

Tour in eagles.

I couldn't wait to go to the next tournament but Ellen wouldn't allow it because she had set up a series of tests to find out what was going on in the body of one Ken Green. They found nothing out of the ordinary and I never got to find out if I could've gone 3-3.

1988 Dunlop Phoenix

I was fortunate enough to be invited to go to Japan to play in the Dunlop Phoenix- in their eyes a major championship- for four years. In 1988 I was coming off my best year so I was still pretty psyched to have a chance to win the Dunlop Phoenix and the richest purse in golf. I loved the course in Miyazaki, which is near the southern end of Japan. It was a tree-lined golf course with smaller greens. My wife Ellen and cousin/caddie Joe LaCava were there with me.

My newborn son Hunter was also in attendance, but he didn't know it because he was only a few months old. I got off to a good start the first two days but was not leading. I then played well on Saturday and assumed the lead. Right on my cute ass were some no-names, including Fred Couples, who was paired with me. In the group in front was Seve Ballesteros and Tom Watson, I think. Tom didn't play well the last day so faded off quickly as he flew his driver all over the place.

We were going back and forth on this tricky track and with four holes to go I had managed to pull ahead by a shot. Fifteen through seventeen were pretty serious holes. I recall doing a brutal up-and-down for pars on all three holes with the one on 17 being a sand save that, quite honestly, only me or the guy in front of me could've up-and-downed. (Ironically, I had just watched Seve miss his up-and-down from that exact position in front of me).

The last hole was a par-5 with trees all over the place. I smoked my drive down the middle but knew this hole was only a 'maybe' for me to go for in two shots. I knew Freddie could go for it because he was twenty yards or so longer but he hit his tee shot so far right it was closer to Hawaii than the fairway.

I would like to tell you that I made a miraculous shot to win, but Seve failed to birdie the hole and Freddie made bogey so I just played the hole safely to win my third event that year. I won $225,000 which, like I said, was massive back then. I also won a car, which gave me an additional $45,000, so it was a great way to finish off what would be my best year on tour. It's funny because technically this was my most competitive event against superstars but many don't count it as a big win because it was in Japan. I however, know it was just as hard to win against those great players as in the USA. I won the world-wide money list title that year although it didn't exist back then like it does now.

I'm going to say something I probably shouldn't so just take it as fact and not that I'm insulting America: I respect the so-called 'average' employee over in Japan immensely. The course we played had two ladies whose sole job was to take care of each hole to perfection. They made sure nothing was out of place- weeds, torn pieces of grass, the bunker, and leaves falling off trees, were all tidied up immediately. They were diligent and proud of their work. Sadly, myself included, Americans might have looked at this job as bullshit and only done a half-assed job of it. I learned a valuable lesson over there: If you're going to do it, do it to your best possible abilities.

1989 Greater Greensboro Open

Going back to Greensboro, North Carolina, was always fun. I had a good history at Forest Oaks, plus I knew the Hodgin family who were like my second mom and dad. I met Norm Hodgin in a Monday pro-am, and he was a happy-go-lucky Carolina boy with a great wife, Libby, who watched us play all day. I was really impressed by how close the whole family was with each other. It was great fun hanging out, playing whiffle ball and drinking beers, which made the week just seem like I was home with my family and friends. This year I was more excited than usual because I had lost in a playoff the year before to Sandy Lyle. It stung, but golf does that to you a lot.

I fired off a 66 Friday and Saturday and was leading going into the last round. I was pretty intense because I kind of had a mission to accomplish but I was also very confident because the course just fit my eye. I'd like to tell you that it got close, or that I was panicking, but truth be told it was mine to win or lose.

I played well on the front and two quick birdies on the back basically put it in the Don't Screw This Up mode, which I didn't. I had avenged a tough loss from the year before. It was a really good feeling. The after-party with my new family was very special to me as well. I didn't know this at the time, but in a decade or so I would end up marrying their daughter Jeannie, whom I loved dearly until the day I lost her. I really think that having the Hodgin family there made the event so much easier and enjoyable for me.

1990 Hong Kong

We've certainly laughed by now at the infamous 'green sauce' poured over my head on a plane at the Miami airport. I will have to admit though that once we arrived to the tournament Ellen was really very good. She was making her debut as a caddie too, which was comical for sure. She pulled a golf cart around all week.

There was a big practice round skins game the Tuesday before the tournament where Bernhard Langer, Isao Aoki (I think), I, and a local stud battled it out. The round was packed with spectators which was fun as hell because of the excitement and the intrigue of whether the local guy could beat the other three studs. Very few skins were out by the time we got to the 18th hole- it was a nine-hole carry over and pretty much whoever would win the next skin would be the big winner. There was close to $90,000 up for grabs, which is big bucks now but then was *really* big bucks.

The last hole there is a beast. It was about 450 yards and tight off the tee. The usually unflappable Langer pull-forked his drive into the trees and was done for the hole. Aoki hit a mini slice into the right trees which eliminated him. Now it was the local hero versus the green shoes and gloved me.

We both hit perfect tee shots which left me with about 180 yards to the pin. The local hero hit first but hit it a tad thin and came up just short of the green. I figured he should be able to make par unless he blows his chip. I proceeded to hit a complete push 5-iron which hit the wrong side of the green and rolled even farther away than its original 40 feet. After it stopped rolling down the slope I was left with a 75-footer with a 7-foot break from right to left. I figured there was a better than even chance I two-putt for par and about the same for him. He pitched up to about four feet, leaving him an envious straight uphill putt. Short and straight, uphill.

For just such an occasion I have my *hit, hope and pray* stroke, which I unleashed on this 75-footer. The ball rolled for what seemed like forever and then out of nowhere, dropped into the hole. The huge crowd was stunned. It went completely silent, even though I had made an enormous putt. Then it was like a light went off and the crowd realized they needed to applaud. It was a wild sensation, feeling like I had just cut the hero's throat. I felt bad but I got over it quickly.

That night we attended a special dinner with the sponsor. I was my usual well-mannered soul when suddenly they bring out two buckets. *What the hell is going on here?* I wonder. Is this payback for beating their local hero? Are they going to douse me with cow turds or spittoon remnants? They explain to me that I'm the guest of honor so I get to pick out the fish. I'm like *Shit, I can't do this.* These poor bastards are flopping around all over wondering what's going on and I'm supposed to choose which ones to put to death? I swallowed my pride and ego and picked out the poor bastard, which I can still see and remember to this day.

The first two days were filled with terrible weather and I didn't play exceptionally well but the scores weren't low so I was definitely in the tournament. After a really good Saturday round I was now leading by one. The closest anyone came to me was when Ellen came inches from rolling over my ball with the pull cart. The two-shot penalty would've made it close, but I literally stopped her right before contact. We laughed and I won the event easily with a good last round. I'm really proud of how I've finished in my events. The biggest unknown in golf is why some guys close well and others seem to just shit the bed under the gun. I don't have the answer except that I just don't panic. I just won't stop grinding it out until it's over and I'm the low guy. I've led or tied for the lead eight times and every time I either won or finished with the low score. I lost Westchester in a playoff one year after being tied. So, maybe I did have that Jack or Tiger gene when it came to clutch golf. I just wasn't as good as they were so I wasn't in contention as much as they were.

11/

Reputation

I was known for having a spirited temper on tour. Basically I got pissed off when I screwed up. But no matter how upset I was, the only objects of my fury were me, my clubs, and my bag. I would never berate or yell at my caddie or any of the volunteer marshals (unlike the majority of PGA Tour players) and I would never refuse to give autographs (see Exception One, Chapter 12).

My putters took the brunt of my spirited behavior. I have so many Ping N-Echo's scattered all over the world. *USA Today* once did a map highlighting where each one of my putters had died in a body of water where I laid it to rest. I have putters in the Pacific and Atlantic along with ponds and lakes all over. I'm talking Pebble, Hawaii, Arizona, Texas, Florida, New York, Connecticut, Michigan and god knows where else. Any course with water, really. Many people know the famous 17th hole (the "island green") at the TPC Stadium Course where we play the Players Championship every year. I had made the cut but my N-Echo was talking back to me a lot so I was very mature and calmly told her that if she didn't start behaving she was going to die.

As we all know, putters don't listen very well. I had warned her, for Pete's sake, but she still wasn't paying attention, so I devised a way to terminate our relationship without being convicted and fined.

So on the 17th, before putting out, I sauntered over to my caddie and good friend Eric Larson.

"I want you to stand over by the edge of the greenside bunker. After I putt out I'm going to toss the putter to you with some juice behind it. I need you to pretend to reach for it but let it go," I explained, like a General speaking to his single troop. He looked at me sideways and then nodded. He knew me, as any good caddie should.

I was playing with Don Pooley that day, who is my polar opposite when it comes to emotion. If you parked a car on Don Pooley he would politely recommend you have your tires examined for wear. So I holed out my putt and then turned and heaved a perfect bullet just over my caddie's head where he then earned an imaginary Oscar by reaching for it like Willie Mays. He then of course let it fly into the 17th pond at the TPC.

The crowd went into *ooh* and *ahh* mode. As we were walking off the green I turned to Don.

"Don, did you see Eric just let that putter go on purpose? What was he thinking?"

Don looked over at Eric as though he were Jack the Ripper. The entire 18th hole he kept giving E the look of shock at letting his man down. You see, I knew I was going to get turned in by someone so I had to have a plan for my defense, and that was that my caddie simply screwed up. The tour knew I would toss my clubs to my caddies all the time, whether it was a brutal shot or a great shot.

One week later I received my fine taped to my locker. I then proceeded to explain my story of total innocence and that if they needed corroborating evidence they could check with Eric and Pooley to verify the accidental death of PING-N-Echo 26. A couple weeks later I received a letter rescinding my fine. It's amazing how much trouble and effort I go through to get out of trouble.

Regardless of my herculean efforts at not taking responsibility for my actions, I was still getting fined left and right from 1989 to 1993. Some were justified for sure, but a lot were just total BS.

I'm in Japan one year at the Dunlop Phoenix (their flagship event in Japan) and we're in the player lounge screwing around when I see Lanny Wadkins and Craig Stadler sitting at a table munching on respective Milky Way bars. Stads is known for burying clubs into the ground left and right. He made *me* look like Don Pooley. I sauntered over to him.

"Stads, how many times have you been fined?"

Stads looks at me and starts to run things through his head, counting, I assume. He then looks at me and says, "I've never been fined."

"What?!" I said. "How the hell does that happen with all you've done?" I implored. He just laughed his fat ass off at me.

Damn, I think.

"Ok Lanny, you're a verbal nightmare and you deliver beat-downs on your clubs regularly. Clearly you've been fined up the pa-tootie, right?" I ask Wadkins.

He thinks for a second, then looks up with a sly-ass smile. *No fucking way*, I think. He read the increasingly pained expression on my face.

"Calm down Ken, I have in fact been fined," he replied, having added up all the times in his head, I'm guessing.

"I've been fined about thirty times," I confessed.

"I got fined once, but I deserved it," Lanny finally revealed.

Oh good, that's great, thanks Lanny.

My reputation of being an angry soul but a great interview was due to the fact that I said things like I believed them to be. In those days however, players never really said what they wanted—they all played the cookie-cutter role to perfection.

Now here's the twist: I swear to you on my dogs' life that I was holding back *every single time*. In my tiny brain I thought I was being good and proper. If I had said what I really wanted to say I guess I would've been suspended for life. And now I kind of am anyway. Guess I shouldn't have held back at all.

12/

Best and Worst Autographs

My favorite place on golfing earth is Pebble Beach Golf Links in Pebble Beach, California. I mean, it's a course that couldn't be built today due to the nutjobs at the EPA. I've divorced Pebble more times than I've been divorced in real life. The 1980-99 era was not the most friendly, putting surface-wise; wet and bumpy, with spike marks bigger than Bob Hope's nose. It was a fluke if you made anything over five feet. Every year I would do my best Ken Green pissing-and-moaning act. *You dumbass MF idiot why the hell did you agree to play this damn course? This is the last time- I'm never going back, ever again.* Then five minutes before the commitment time ended the following year I would sign up again. Pure love-hate with those greens.

Once again this one year I committed to play on the Friday before tourney week and by the following Saturday afternoon I'm swearing my ass off once again, cussing myself out for playing there. This particular year I'm missing the cut and am finishing on the gorgeous ninth at Pebble. Earlier, on the sixth hole, I decided I was going to deep-six my PING-N-Echo into the Pacific, never to be seen again. On the ninth green I casually putted out first and strolled quietly to the edge of the cliff where the putter would soon be executed. Once the last guy putted out I unwound and hummed that puppy as far as I could. It had to clear the beach down below, which was a decent piece of real estate, I'm telling you. It flew into the ocean easily. As I watched it splash into the ocean rollers it was still screaming at me. I guessed it was a good 10 yards into the ocean and had drowned as any traitor should. I was relieved knowing my stupid ass wasn't coming back for many years. This time it was personal.

Next February rolls along and sure as sugar I sign up once again on the Friday before tournament week. I'm enjoying myself this year when a couple strolls up to me and asks if I would mind signing an autograph. "Love to," I said as they pulled out this big 11" x 14" photograph. The photo was of the husband a little more than waist deep in the ocean with this huge smile on his face and his hands held high, brandishing my now-departed PING-N-Echo putter. They then told me the story that they had been waiting all year to tell me- they had seen me execute my putter and felt they had no choice but to go save it from its watery grave. Apparently it took him about 45 minutes to find it. It's my favorite autograph story- an absolute classic you would be hard to top on any tour worldwide.

Now I'm not sure how many other pros have a favorite, or even a least favorite, story about autographs but I refuse to tell you a great one without telling you the one I regret the most. Castle Pines Country Club in the Denver area was a great stop for us and a favorite of mine as I won the inaugural The International in 1986. Sometime in the early 1990s I was playing well but had managed to throw away about $30,000 with a nice double-bogey on the last hole. Some of you know I had (had!) a nice temper at times and you can only imagine how pissed I was at throwing away the value of a decent sports car in about eight minutes. These were the days when we had a small corridor of ropes where fans would hang out and ask for autographs.

Despite me wanting to go through my bag and snap every club I owned, I signed all the autographs for everyone in the autograph area. I finally finished and scowled off into the blocked-out Players Only area. I was about to walk into the clubhouse when this guy jumped over the ropes and ran to me saying he really wanted my autograph. I gave him some shit about jumping over the ropes and told him to get the hell away. I regret this immensely to this day, as you can see. If you're still alive and reading this sir, I'm really sorry, I was dead wrong.

I won my first event at the Buick Open in Grand Blanc, Michigan in August of 1985. I had committed to play in the John Deforest pro-am the next day in the Catskills. John was a friend and even though I had parties to attend Sunday night I was going to take the first flight out Monday morning with zero sleep due to a flood of testosterone as you might imagine. I showed up and had a good day where I met a young girl named Angela who followed us around. I chatted with the twelve-year-old as much as I could but the day ended and off I drove to Doug Ramey's house for my party-with-friends celebration, which became a winning week tradition.

When I showed up the next year at John's tournament Angela was there and she gave me the most cherished gift I've ever received from a fan. She had saved up her allowance money to buy me a tie clip which she had engraved with my name. I just thought that was the best gift I could ever receive. I wore that tie clip every tour round for years until I lost it. I was once again at my friends' house for our 'automatic' victory party on a Monday following a win. Somehow I managed to get into an argument with my girlfriend and as we were leaving she swung at me and managed to knock the tie clip off my shirt without me noticing. By the time I realized it was gone I had left Danbury. Sadly my friend never found it. To this day it's something I remember often and miss. It's the best gift a young man could ever have received and I will always remember it fondly. Thank you Angela.

13/

Q School

I was about out of fight and out of money. The divorce with Save-ra had worn me down enough to the point where I had lost my playing privileges on the PGA Tour. On tour, either you make enough money from the previous year to keep or get your tour card (a term indicating you're a card-carrying member of the PGA Tour) or you go to the PGA Tour Qualifying Tournament, otherwise known as "Q School." It's agreed universally that this event is one of the most terrifying, nerve-wracking and difficult experiences in pro golf. Many pros say they would rather have a half-dozen root canals than go through the stress of Q School.

The 1984 Q School was at the TPC Stadium Course. You can only imagine trying to get your card by having to play what was then known as the hardest golf course in America, if not the world. I would watch and see the fear in everyone's eyes. I was calm and mildly sea-soned at that point and knew I was going to get my card back at Q School, but that didn't mean it was easy.

For our sixth and final round I was playing with Doug Black, who was great to play with. We both started the day in the middle of the pack (around 25th) but at that course you can't fall asleep. Doug played phenomenally through 15 holes, two or three under par, and he could have won the whole thing. He finished double bogey, quadruple bogey, triple bogey and we literally never heard from him again. Such is pro golf.

At 16 I snap-hooked my tee shot into the woods and punched out into the fairway, and then hit a 1-iron to about 15 feet and made the putt on a thin, three-tiered green (which they have since de-clawed to make it easier for players to make eagle). I went birdie, par, par, and moved up 15 spots in the tournament.

Q School made you do strange things—it messed with your head. In Palm Springs in 1982, we're playing at La Quinta on the Mountain Course, where the 17th hole is a seriously tight driving hole where you should never use driver, and then a second shot over water. Of course I hit driver. In this particular case I smoked it and all that was left was a 9-iron to the pin, at least that's what I'm thinking when I walk off the tee toward my ball.

I get to the ball and start doing my yardage to the hole. It tells me 135 yards to carry the water and 165 yards to the pin. *165 yards?* That's not a 9-iron, that's a 6-iron. I redo the yardage: 165 yards. I redo it. 165 yards. I can't believe what I'm seeing. I had absolutely striped the drive right down the middle but still have a 6-iron to the hole? I pull out the 6-iron and hit the absolute worst shot of my career, totally laying the sod over it. The ball barely flew the water, clearing the railroad ties at the front of the green by inches and rolled more than 80 feet to within 15 feet of the hole. I'm flabbergasted. I absolutely chunked it and the ball still rolled to within 15 feet. I did the yardage again and low and behold, it told me it was 105 to the front and 135 to the pin, or a 9-iron. I had checked the yardage three times and got the wrong yardage and I kept saying, "This is the wrong yardage," but my nerves kept interrupting and I panicked and messed up my yardage every single time.

Bob Tway, who at Oklahoma State was one of the best college players of all time, blew it coming down the stretch on his first two attempts to get his card. He had to sit out two years because he couldn't make it past Q School.

The first time I got my card was in Brownsville, Texas. They had a par-3 there that was 220 yards and dead over water, and while the green technically wasn't an island, it was. I hit it in the water every day the first three days. The last day I'm already thinking about this hole on the front nine. I get to this hole and it was a gift from heaven—they moved the tee up so that instead of a 1-iron it was a 7-iron.

Playing the last hole, a par-5, all I needed was par to get my card. Of course I aggressively go for the green in two but I pull it left into a bunker. So now I have the hardest shot in golf: the 50-yard bunker shot. I was so scared I would mess it up that I took out an 8-iron and chipped it out to about 20 feet from the pin, two-putted and got my card. Looking back it was absolutely the wrong decision to try to pick an 8-iron off the sand than to hit an explosion shot. After all, the whole purpose of exploding the ball from the sand is so you don't have to pick it, which is much more difficult. That was a terrible shot choice. But that's what Q School did to you. It turned you into a moron.

I made $42,000 on the PGA Tour in 1983 to finish 114th on the money list. Today 114th on the money list gets you $900,000 in winnings.

But now that I had my card, which really was the hard part, I had to find a way to pay for being out on tour. While the tour does as good a job as they can to keep the tournaments in close proximity from week to week, the bottom line is that playing pro golf, just being out on tour, is a very expensive proposition. Not only are hotels and flights and meals expensive, but there is the caddie to pay, the entry fees to pay and the living expenses beyond the basics. Today, a player who gets his card can be guaranteed a minimum of $250,000 just from sponsors alone, but 30 years ago that wasn't the case. And so I was one broke puppy trying to figure out how I was going to afford the upcoming season. I was wondering if this was all going to be worth it.

The first three years I was on tour I was fortunate to have my uncle Jack Green and other local Danburians sponsor me, and I will never, ever forget that. Back in the day, in fact even today at times, members of local golf clubs (usually from the club that the newly minted pro golfer played out of) would get together to throw a couple thousand dollars each into a pot to help a young local pro play on one of the Tours. In some cases the syndicate of 'investors' would even get an ownership stake in the future earnings of the pro, as any normal investor would. It was a great way for new pros to afford to go on tour while it gave financially gifted weekend golfers an investment in a real-life PGA Tour professional. The amateurs had bragging rights and access to a PGA Tour pro (and all those free instruction tips!) and the pro could afford to get to as many tournaments as he felt comfortable entering.

At this point in my career however, my past sponsors felt it was time to move on and I completely understood. I tried for months to find replacement sponsors but had no luck. So here it is January, and the tour is starting up in two weeks. I was desperate. I had no money to pay for going out there. So me being the delusional genius I am, I decided I would try my luck betting on pro basketball games, something I knew absolutely nothing about. Over the course of one week—and not a word of this is a lie- I bet and won 23 of 24 games. My initial bet of $200 ended with a windfall of $15,000, which was more than enough to get me started on tour.

So on a cold day in November my friends decided to throw me a congratulatory dinner for getting back on tour. I really had the best friends on earth and am blessed that to this day I still have them. The party was at the El Dorado restaurant which had the best Italian food in Danbury. It was also one of our hangouts where after a few cocktails we often ended our night in the parking lot playing "Wallball."

There was an old, empty warehouse on the other end of the massive restaurant parking lot. We split into teams and the goal was to hit golf balls off the warehouse wall 200 yards away and then catch the screaming ball as it came back almost as fast as it had left (that's when we didn't accidentally miss the entire warehouse!). To add to the ridiculousness of these late-night shenanigans, USA Golf Pro Kenneth Green was required to hit his ball off of the width of a quarter—yes, a 25-cent piece. Inexplicably, not once did my special Louise Suggs persimmon driver ever get scratched. The other guys would stick a tee into the cracks of the parking lot. It was a blast.

I arrived at the El Dorado and walked into the dining room but didn't see any of my friends. I checked my watch to see if I was late or too early. I walked through the dining room and into the main room and was suddenly overwhelmed by the welcoming roar from my friends. The place was filled with so many people, from old friends to new ones, and the love in the air was palpable. My cousin Robin was there with her best friend Sue Doceti, who happened to be the most beautiful girl I had ever seen. After making my way around the room thanking everyone for coming, I eventually got the nerve to walk over to Sue.

She was stunning. Her beauty just blew my mind. We had a short but good chat and I asked her out. We set the date up for the following week, seven days hence. The entire next week I was wondering how I could even be in the same room with a girl as gorgeous as Sue. *'What chance do I have with a girl like this?'* I thought almost every minute of the days leading up to our date. As you have no doubt figured out, I'm a complete mess when it comes to women and relationships in general terms- I had no idea how I was going to make this work with a beauty of her caliber. What I didn't know would have made all my worries disappear; Ms. Sue Doceti had a crush on me.

Three days later I had a date with Ellen. She was fun and seemed to genuinely like me. I asked her out again, but she wasn't available except for the day of the date I had arranged with Sue. Never believing that Sue would be into me, I canceled on her and went out with Ellen again. It was the biggest and most costly mistake of my life, bar none.

14/

Reminiscences of the Tour

HAWAII, OAHU - RIP Ken Green 1958-1988

In 1998 we brought Ellen of Medusa's whole family along to Hawaii. I was more than happy to do this ("happy wife, happy life").

Early in the week we decided to have the dreaded "all day" day, which meant sightseeing from sun-up to after sundown. All day went into all night, and we finally dragged our tired tails back to the hotel room at 1am. I eventually noticed the telephone message light on, so I checked it. It said I had 36 messages. I feared that someone in my family had died or was in a bad accident. The first bunch of messages were from reporters asking me if I was well and would I please call them. After listening to a few of them I began to wonder what the heck was going on. Reporters weren't exactly tracking me down on a daily basis. I then got to one that said, "Ken, if you're alive and not dead, you need to call me because it's being reported you were killed in an accident." Little did he know I don't die easily.

I finally reached someone and was told that a helicopter went down over Oahu and there was a "Ken Green" on board, who had died. So earlier in the day, when literally 15 hours went by and not one soul had heard from me or anyone else in my family, they all went into early mourning. Grim messages had my mom in tears for hours, I was later told. My premature death was even announced in the paper the next day since the story went to press before anyone had heard from me. It's kind of wild to be considered dead when in reality you're in your hotel room scratching your belly in your underwear.

KEN GREEN UFC DEBUT

My first trip to the Hawaiian Open with Ellen was more than memorable. Mark Calcavecchia and I decided we would play a practice round at 6:30am and be back to the hotel by 10am at the latest. So that morning I woke and started to get ready. I told Medusa that I would be back in a few hours. I said we would then take the kids and do some kid things. Mind you, we spent all day Monday doing kids' stuff. But that didn't fly and Ellen went ballistic, saying I needed to grow up, be a real dad, and every other thing she could think of. After about 15 minutes I said "enough," and that I would be back by 10am. I walked out the door and was walking down the hall in a complete state of shock. Just before I reached the elevator I took an Ellen right hook to the kisser. I mean, I was stunned. I now had blood all over my face and shirt. I shook my head, didn't say a word, walked back into the hotel room and washed up. Then I left again.

I was now a little late to meet Calc so was trying to hurry up. When I met him he took one look at me and said, "Green, what the fuck happened?"

"Oh, just had a few issues, all's good now, let's go hit 'em," I replied.

But Calc wasn't moving.

"Green, take a look at your shirt," he said as he looked at me incredulously.

I looked down and I had the same shirt on, with all the blood splatter. I swear I thought I had changed it. Obviously not. It was the new bloody tie-dye.

"Green, what the hell happened to your glasses," he said, pointing to my face. I pulled the glasses off and they were all bent and crooked. I guess in my shock I never noticed that either. I then spit the story out. He didn't stop laughing all day.

Punches thrown: 0, Punches taken: 1. Medusa wins unanimously. If I had half a brain I would've walked away, as it was the first of many signs I just blocked out. It wasn't my last TKO.

KAPALUA - THE BERMUDA TRIANGLE

Try to remember, these were the days of old Bermuda grass and its dreaded grain. For those of you old enough, you know how hard it was to read and putt on that stuff–*impossible*. There's a reason Tom Watson never won in Florida, by God. Now try and imagine: This place is Bermuda and it's grain-on-steroids. The young studs of today have no idea how lucky they are to be putting on this new stuff. Half of them would have quit the game of golf if they had to contend with Bermuda greens.

So in Kapalua about six of us would get up and tee off around 6 a.m. and play 27 holes. One of the days Calc and I took on Andy Bean and Ben Crenshaw. Bean made more putts on this track than possible, and we made diddly squat. I can't tell you how many times we swore at Bean that day but the number is voluminous. A few thousand dollars later we found ourselves having lunch. My caddie and great friend Eric Larson and I were going to play tennis that afternoon, and Bean started rubbing it in even more by saying he and his partner would bury us on the court. Fork you, you big-ass redneck! Match on. I'm happy to report that I got half of my losses back, but the memory I cherish most was the "skins" I earned. Bean didn't know it but we played tennis with an add-on rule of hitting the guy on the other side—thereby scoring a "skin." My first skin was a nice bullet overhead that smacked him right in the chest. Because it was a jumping overhead he took it in stride, not thinking I was trying to ping him. It was, after all, a fluke shot. The next skin was the skin of all skins. It was a mishit shot that floated to my right, and I ran it down for a bullet-return straight into his nuts. Bean goes down like a Georgia Pine- *timber!* A great memory, I tell you.

MARK VIII

They were giving away a Lincoln Mark VIII for the closest to the pin on the 18th at Kapalua. If you know the hole, it's a monster par-5, dead downhill and turns hard left the last 60 yards. I tell you this because back then I couldn't hit a draw to save my life. On top of that, the shot was on a severe downhill lie, so I'm doomed.

I told my boy E Larson that if I pulled the shot off and won the car, he could have it. Well dear me, I pulled off the flukiest pull-draw ripped 3-iron that hooked left at the bend and bounced 40 yards to the front and then rolls onto the green where the puppy goes another 35 yards and stops five feet from the hole. I'm the best, damn it! And since I'm a man of my word I give the car to E. That is until Medusa finds out about it and goes berserk. She tells me it's nuts to give my caddie a $40,000 car.

We already had two new cars, and we definitely didn't need another one. Eric said, "Green, don't worry about it, I know how Eleanor is (he called her Eleanor) when she becomes the evil demon." But I wasn't having it.

Back and forth we went, and I held my own for a day or two… and then melted like Chunky Monkey in the Sudan. Her final point, the one where I knew I was doomed, was when she said we had to save the car for Brad to drive when he turned 16. I looked at her in disbelief, but knew the fight was lost. Brad was six-years-old.

FOUR!

Some of you may have heard about my tendency to create and play golf in some really bizarre places. I design courses that only the real man can play. The real *stupid* man, that is. This particular night in Honolulu I designed the Club of Pool: from the middle of the hotel room, out the sliding door, across the road to the pool on the roof of the hotel across the street. This was one of the trickier shots, I tell you. I think it must have been the nightly changing winds that never allowed me to make even one. Not a one, damn it! The distance was about 200 yards and that week I emptied a bag of range balls trying to sink it. What made this shot so hard was that you had to make sure you hit it high enough to get over the balcony fence, but not too high to hit the top of roof. I failed. Sometimes you have to just live with your failures and move on.

MOLOKAI

Sister Shell and I were visiting a friend who stayed in Molokai, Hawaii for months in the winter. It was a great way to spend a month and veg out. 'Vegging out' for me was playing golf in the early morning and then doing whatever in the afternoon. This afternoon, sis wanted to hang out at the beach for a while. I boogie-boarded for a bit in the great waves and then called it a day. Shelley decided to go back out and goof around in the surf. I sat on the beach enjoying the Hawaiian scenery when I looked out and noticed that Shelley seemed to be in a panic. A deadly rip tide apparently had gotten her and I ran into the surf and swam out to her as fast as my hunky body would move. When I reached her she was struggling to stay afloat and in her panic her asthma had kicked in, so now her breathing was getting really hard. Being the brain-damaged soul I am, I foolishly decided to calm her and just tell her I was going to grab her. I had no clue if we indeed were in a mini-riptide, or just big-ass waves, unable to swim back. All I knew for sure that if I didn't pull this off we were both going to die.

"I won't let anything happen to you, just trust me," I said, my voice shaking. I know for a fact that the only reason we made it back without drowning was because of my Guides, God, or the Universe of Souls. To this day I have no idea how we made it. If she knew how scared I was and that I knew we were surely going to die, she would've really panicked. To this day she won't touch the ocean or bodies of water.

PEBBLE BEACH - KEN & CAT MAKE HEADLINES

The year was 1983 at my favorite place on U.S. soil. I shot a 66 at Spyglass Hill, which back then was scary low. This was in my view the hardest course we play all year. If Spyglass was set up like the majors or some other events, the scores would be over par. The 66 was a course record, so that will tell you how hard the track is.

I was leading my first event after 36 holes on the PGA Tour! In the press tent they were trying to figure out who this studly-looking dude was and what made him tick. Me being me, I mentioned that due to having a serious budget shortfall I was staying down on what I called, "Oh Shit Row." I didn't give a flying hoot because I was playing on the tour and would sleep on the sidewalk if I had to.

That week I mentioned how I had adopted a roommate, an orange tabby cat. I was buying food and feeding it all week, and after a few days I finally convinced my new little buddy to hang out with me in the room. She was in heaven, but like all females she liked to go out in the middle of the night and party. Unlike some girls however, she actually wanted to come back when she was done. The dilemma, which I solved easily, was how the cat was going to get back into the room. So I simply left the door open. Did I tell you I have brain damage? Here we are in a not-so-nice neighborhood, and I leave my room open for a stray cat. The media was flipping out that I would do such a thing *down there*, of all places. One reporter wanted to see proof that I was sleeping with such a fine feline. He came, he saw, he believed. We both had our picture in the paper the next day. I so wish I had saved that article. Brain damage! When I left, I gave the front desk girl $300 and asked her to please feed her. I hope she did.

Oh by the way, for the third round I was at the infamous Cypress Point. It rained all day long, not a downpour but just your basic hard-core Monterey drizzle. I started the day in first, and shot a 71, which to be truthful, I was pleased with. I even had to hit driver off 16, the killer par-3 over the Pacific Ocean. Jack lays up most of the time! I hit the green and made par too. When I finished, I found out Tom Kite picked off a mere 62 at Pebble and was the new leader. Shit! Welcome to the PGA Tour. I don't recall how many back I was, but it was too far to catch him. Another piss poor day on Sunday, along with a so-so round of 76, gave me a tie for 7th and my first Top 10. When you don't fall off the first page of the leaderboard after a 76, that tells you all you need to know about how hard it was that day.

HALL SEX

There was a pro event called the Spalding Invitational that included many PGA Tour pros and LPGA players, along with some club pros. It was an unofficial event, but I won it in 1986 for my second win. The following year I brought out my friends Eric Larson and Jack Garamella, who also was my Connecticut attorney. This was pro-am style for the first three days on three different courses, and then on the fourth day only the pros played. This was a fun event for my friends and a way for me to repay their friendship by bringing them. But this changed when Medusa decided to be Medusa once again.

Ellen elected not to go out and have dinner with the rest of us. We stayed out way too late. Everyone was hammered, and I was a little tipsy but not awful because I was there for both fun and golf, so I had to keep my wits about me.

Joe LaCava, my cousin and caddie at the time, was sharing a room with Eric Larson. When we all arrived back to the hotel, Ellen refused to let me in the room. So I did what any normal guy would do. I walked two rooms down and banged on Joe and E's room. After banging for 15 minutes, I had to admit these boys were out cold. So I then skipped on down to the front desk where I was going to get a key to my room. Well, I didn't have my ID on me, it was in the room. So they called up to the room to see if the person therein could vouch for me. Ellen told the front desk she had no idea who I was. Then they called the other room, with the sleeping drunks, but that was pointless. So I skipped-a-do back upstairs and went to sleep in the hall.

The collective woke up for our third round as I lay in the hallway, asking why in a pig's ear I was there. Much laughter later, I washed up in their room and was ready to go. When I walked out the door Ellen happened to walk by with her luggage, said, "Fuck you," and then flew off to San Francisco. I was wondering what was going on but didn't have time to mess with it since I was already late leaving for round three of the Spalding.

I played well on Saturday and was in the last group going into the final round. It was a grind and very close. On 16 I hit it in the deep right-greenside bunker where I was just able to see the pin. I took a look up over the lip, and then flinched. I stepped away from the ball. There, standing directly behind the pin behind the green, I saw Medusa. She was obviously back from her two-day disappearance.

I had real trouble regrouping, but I knew if I don't make par it was over, since I was two back. I hit a WOW shot, and stopped the ball within four feet, which I'm telling you was amazing. Then I made the putt. *Still hope*, I thought. *Forget her and get moving*, I told myself.

I birdied 17 with a nice 15-footer. On 18 I stuffed an 8-iron to two feet and made the putt to get into a three-way playoff.

On the first playoff hole we all hit good tee shots and I was walking down the left side of the ropes chatting with my caddie E. I walked ahead and then I heard Ellen: "Kenny, Kenny come here," she said, waving me over. I walked over and she gave me a kiss on the cheek to show the crowd her support, or to show me she was the one in control. Stunned, I completely flailed my 5-iron and pushed the crap out of it. It was a back left pin and I was in a short, right bunker, with a 40-yard bunker shot to stay in the playoff. The closest shot was 40 feet, so I was thinking if I could somehow pull off one of the harder shots in golf, I have a chance. I hit a classic to 3 feet.

Then, onto the next hole and *Ooops*, Lennie Clements makes a 40-footer and shit it's all over. As I was walking back to the clubhouse in a daze Ellen walks up and grabs my hand. I have no idea why I didn't stick the putter up her ass.

PEBBLE

The very first year of the Tour Championship was in 1988, and we were at Pebble, which at the end of the year is usually much firmer and thus nicer. That year three of us had a chance to be the first player to earn over a million dollars for the year. (Tell me I'm not pissed

I wasn't born much later, as they're winning a million-plus for one event now.) So Curtis Strange, Tom Kite, and I were the three with a chance at the million-dollar year. We were all in it going into the final round. I started a couple back from them when a classic storm-from-hell came as I was on the 8th (remember, we didn't have the ability to see accurately what storms were coming, back then). I couldn't get home on 9 with the wind dead in my face, but managed par. The rain was coming down pretty hard and the wind was blowing 30mph-plus. On the 10th I hit driver and was about 10 yards short of the green. More brain damage! How on earth do you hit driver off the deck on a hard left-to-right slope where there is nothing but ocean on your right? The rain was now bad-ass and going straight sideways. Tour official Mike Shea was right next to the green and I went over and said, "We can't play in this stuff, when are you going to pull us off?"

He said we would keep going.

I hit my pitch to 18 inches and when it was my turn to putt I stepped up to make an ordinary stroke. As I did a big blast of wind literally knocked me off my feet and I barely hit the ball. I missed the hole by a foot. Think about that: I missed an 18-inch putt by 12 inches. I somehow managed to get the next one in the hole, and right after I did, they blew the damned horn. I've never been so pissed in my life.

After the break we went back out. I finished one back of both Kite and Strange. I'm not saying I would've won the playoff, but damn it, I should've been there. Bad luck you say? Maybe, but this was also the time where I signed on with PING during the square groove issue and I was the leper. Was it intentional on the tour's part? I'll never know. Strange won the playoff. I did end up having the most world-wide earnings, official and unofficial, than anyone that year. So, I did hold a mini-record for a while, and for that I can always smile inside.

LOOP AT PEBBLE

The most peaceful and loving moment I've ever had on a golf course was in 2008 at Pebble. It was about three events into my senior career. I was rusty and clearly getting the golf cobwebs and nerves out of my system. My youngest son Hunter and I were, for the first time in a while, finally having fun times together. I was thrilled to get to know him again. My wife Jeanne was also with us. It was a Tuesday and the course was empty. I played the first 12 holes and I was having back issues, so I told Hunt to head straight down to 10 and play 10-11-12-

13-9 and we'll see what happens after that. Jeanne and I were enjoying ourselves and the calmness of a beautiful day that overlooking the 10th at Pebble can bring you. In an hour Hunter was back and had a smile from ear-to-ear. I asked him how he played and he laughed and said, "Shitty!"

I said, "Go get revenge and do the loop again."

"Really?" he said. I told him to go and play better. I will never forget watching him going down that fairway, bag on shoulder, looking like he had totally forgotten about his troubles. I was in heaven, and I suppose all parents can relate to that moment when you see joy and peace in your child. Before long, he was back again.

Well?

"I'm so close," he said. "So much better," he said.

I said, "Do you think you can do better than what you just did?"

"Hell yeah," he said.

Then go get 'em!

Then, back again, with the biggest smile ever.

"I'm guessing you did better?"

He laughed and said it was the best he ever played any holes, much less the brutality of Pebble. He was one over for 5 holes and Hunt was a 20-handicapper! I would soon lose him, but that's the last memory I have that will never disappear, even though we would spend many more days together before he went home.

JACK & THE U.S. OPEN

The first U.S. Open I qualified for was the '82 Open at Pebble Beach. It was also my first year on tour, so I was pumped to the max. I mean, how cool was it that Pebble would be my first US Open?! Some tour friends and I had made a tee time, but when we showed up there were five of us. Obviously someone was pulling a fast one, but no one copped to it. I then said, "Go ahead I'll find a group somewhere." The starter looked at me and said, "Mr. Green, our tee times are full and I'm not sure I can do much." I shrugged and said, "Let's see what happens."

After twenty minutes of sitting around watching groups tee off, my caddie takes off to go do something- I have no clue what. Right then Lanny Wadkins, Seve Ballesteros, and another player walk up to the tee. The starter notices that their fourth is a no-show and tells them a quick version of the story. He then asks them if they would mind if I joined them. They said absolutely. I was petrified and wanted nothing to do with those studs. I hemmed & hawed and said, "OK, if my caddy gets back with my clubs." I was praying he had been run over by a delivery truck or had fallen into the ocean! Luckily he had and I didn't have to tee off with them. The starter then said, "Geez, Mr. Green, that was a great opportunity and…" he trailed off. I was apologetic and gave him my Sorry Face.

Thirty more minutes passed and a thunder of footsteps were heard coming down to the first tee. I mean, it was like the elk or deer were invading the first tee. I looked up and saw a mob of people all over the place. A tall-ass guy popped out and it was Tom Weiskopf, and I was like, *wow shit.* Then a couple minutes later the people parted and I was dead sure Moses was going to walk up onto the tee. I was wrong, it was God himself, Jack Nicklaus! I thought, *This is an incredible dream come true and I have a front row seat!*

Jack walked up to the starter and said hello, and the starter said hello back. He then asked Jack if he had a tee time. Jack said, no he didn't. The starter quickly said, "You're on the tee!" I thought that was deservedly so. What I heard next almost made me poop my pants.

"Do you have room for young Mr. Green, who needs a game?" asked the starter of the greatest player who ever lived.

No no no! I thought.

Yes yes yes, said Jack.

I had no excuses. I was about to play with Jack effing Nicklaus. I teed up and was standing over the ball and all I could think about was *Please God please tell me they can't see my knees shaking.* They were shaking I'm telling you. I hit what looked like a perfect shot right down the middle. It was a neck-drive that was weak but I was thrilled it actually went in the air and onto the short grass! They were the nicest guys to play with and I can't say enough about how much they talked and would give advice about each hole if I asked.

Well, the crowd had swelled to massive proportions when we went off 14. Jack and Weiskopf playing the US Open at Pebble—what a dream! On the next hole we all hit our tee shots and then Jack disappeared. Tom said not to worry, Jack is a little loose in the head but he'll be back. Before I knew it we were on 16 and I was wondering if we should call the cops or what—still no Jack.

As we walked off the tee, up walks Jack with four peach ice

cream cones- his favorite ice cream, and he knew where they sold it on the course. Think about that for a second. I mean, I had Jack getting me an ice cream cone. I was The Man! By the time we teed off 18 the hole was covered with people. Tom hit a bomb down the middle and Jack then hit a bomb down the left side. Don't ask where I hit it. (Into the ocean). I will say however, that I only hit it one more time into that ocean on the left the rest of my days.

Tom was over the ball and Jack stopped him. He says, "Hey, eagles for dinner?" Tom says sure. He gets over the ball and pulls back. "Wait, you have your whole fucking family out here," Weiskopf says. Jack just smiles. Tom then rips a 3-wood at the right front pin. It flew into the lip of the bunker and rolled to the bottom.

Jack had 252 to the front and proceeded to pull out a 1-iron (an extinct club now). I turned to my caddie and said, "What is he thinking? There is no way in hell he can get there with a 1-iron." Here I am a rookie telling someone that Jack Nicklaus has no idea what he's doing. He then proceeded to hit a high floating bomb and flew it 253 yards. It stopped 40 feet from the pin. That made no sense to me. How could that be done? The roar the crowd made when he made the putt was the loudest I've ever heard in a practice, and many tournaments too. A round of golf I will never forget.

BROTHER BILL & FRIENDS

I'm very lucky to have figured out early in life that my friends and family mean more to me than anything. Well, them and my dogs. For about four years I kept pestering the people at the Crosby to give me an invite to the pro-am so I could bring my brother Bill out there and we could fulfill a dream of sorts. They finally caved, so I coughed up the five grand and off we went. We didn't go without two of my best friends, Greg Begler, aka "Bags," and Doug Ramey, aka "V". We'd known each other since we were in high school and have golfed, drank, and been close ever since. V was going to be Bill's caddie & Bags would loop for me. I was still in the I'm-not-paying-a-bundle-for-hotels, so we stayed on the historic pit road, where you have read about my friendship with the cat a few years back. I had asked V and Bags not to bother the celebs during the pro-am but V refused to listen. We were on the range when suddenly V pulls up with Batman (Michael Keaton) being dragged along by the villain V. He insisted we take a picture with Batman, and luckily for us, Batman was in a good mood and laughed off being batnapped.

Cypress Point was still on the rotation and as luck would have it that was our first tee shot. Tee #1 at Cypress stands at its highest point, so it overlooks the course and the ocean, scattered with some insane houses. It's a classic view, but scary as shit for brother Bill, who is trying to hit the ball forward somehow. Forward it went, though left it also went. It ended up very near the pines and the 14th fairway. He did manage to slap top-it about 40 yards, where he then proceeded to pull-yank another 3-wood just short of the front left bunker. I managed to hit a 6-iron to 5 feet, by the way. The green is 30 feet above where Bill's ball ended up, and he could barely see the pin. He was about to pick it up, and I yelled over to him to give it another whack because you never know. He then proceeded to skull the ball and hit a line drive into the edge of the lip of the bunker, which popped it 50 feet into the air and toward the pin. It flew straight at the flag and dropped right into the hole. I kid you not, this happened just as described. Brother Bill parred the first 5 holes and I birdied the 6th, so we were on top of the damned leaderboard at 6-under through 6! A treasure I will never forget. He never helped me another shot, until he made a par on the great par-3 17th at Pebble, which was 47 holes later. A great time. Oh, by the way, on the 16th, where you hit your shot over 200 yards of the ocean onto the green, the famous of the famous holes at the Point, he hit three into the ocean.

LOS ANGELES- RIVIERA

I love Riviera to death, so I always went every year. Riviera, however, never loved me back. I have no clue whether it was the wacky grass out there or just that we didn't vibe as a couple. After I went four straight years without a birdie and all missed cuts, I pulled a *no mas amigo*. I had to accept that I was just not meant to play there. Somewhere in the late nineties I decided to go back and see if things had changed. I was paired with Jack for the first two days, so that was at least a treat. I birdied the first 3 holes to start my new adventure at Riviera. Holy shit, Jack!

I never saw another birdie and missed yet another cut, and waved the white flag once again. Other than that, I can say that not one interesting thing ever happened there for me.

PHOENIX
I'm sure you have heard the "horses-for-courses," to signify that a player plays a certain course or city very well. I'm here to tell you that if we didn't have 10 weeks off for the winter I might very well never have played the west coast at all. I couldn't play worth a crap on any of those courses, and have no clue why. Was it the whacky grass they had, or was it the time of year, or maybe I was killed in a previous life out there—I just couldn't do squat. I think I had one Top 10 each at Pebble, Phoenix, and Tucson, and only when it was at the end of the year, so that pretty much shows you how pathetic I was out there. I played Phoenix every year because I was a PING player and they always had their little dinner for all the players and I thought it was my obligation to show my gratitude to Karsten and his family. Other than getting lucky once with a volunteer, zippo happened out there too. You have no idea how easy it was to get lucky out there, either with a volunteer or a young lady looking for love, or a sugar daddy.

Calc met his first wife at Phoenix's infamous party tent, the Bird's Nest, close to golf course. My cousin Joe LaCava and Calc decided one night to go over there, and the next thing you know Calc was sucked in by the booby trap of traps. The next day he was in the group right behind me, and they caught us on the fourth tee, and Calc strolled up and waved the girl he'd met over to meet me. What I'm about to say is wrong, and I shouldn't have judged anyone by their appearance, considering I'm not exactly a classy dresser myself, but this girl was wearing these tight jean shorts with a tighter white T-shirt, with one sleeve rolled up holding a pack of cigarettes. It didn't quite fit the golf course, but they did have some good years of marriage. I think.

HONDA AND THE SQUARE GROOVES CONTROVERSY
I started playing The Honda at the infamous Inverrary Country Club, where Jack used to beat the daylights out of people. Then they moved to Eagle Trace, our TPC product. I actually thought Eagle Trace was a nice course. Many of the players thought it was bad, but what they failed to realize was that it was only unfair due to the insane wind we used to get out there near Alligator Alley. Then as technology improved, a greens superintendent by the name of Fred Klauk arrived. He's a nice guy, but has serious demonic issues, I'm telling you. He had those greens so rock-firm that they were off-the-charts difficult

unplayable. In steps the All-Australian egomaniac, Greg Norman, the stud of those days. He complained and bitched so much, saying we would never come back, that they eventually gave in and moved the tourney to Herron Bay, another TPC course. It was a public course and fair at best. The good news is that while Greg got his way, the event didn't get Greg. Despite moving the tournament for the No. 1 player, he only showed up once to my recollection. He just used the excuse of Eagle Trace because he didn't want to play several weeks in a row.

The other notable thing about Eagle Trace was that the square grooves issue came up when Calc hit his infamous shot. He pushed a tee shot into the right rough on No. 16. He then blasted a power 8-iron and flew it right onto the green, about 15 feet away. The ball stopped dead on the green and every player and person who didn't like squares grooves went into attack mode, which eventually lead to the PING lawsuit against the PGA Tour and the USGA. Now, did it ever occur to the powers that be to question Calc? If they did, they might have been told that the reason the ball stopped so fast was because the ball flew into a deep hole. Pure luck started the infamous lawsuit, where I would eventually be shunned by the players because I had the balls to stand with Karsten Solheim and PING.

TOM WATSON AND SQUARE GROOVES
I'll never forget playing with Tom Watson at Pebble Beach. We were just bouncing along until the 15th, which you may remember is the hole that runs with the road. It was Sunday, so the pin was in the typical back right location, which had a brutal right-to-left steep slope and made hitting it close a case of pure luck. Now, me being me- dumb and stupidly aggressive every time I played, I decided I would go right at the pin, which meant I had to hit the ball on the very edge of the right fringe of the green. I stepped right up and smacked a perfect semi-shank, five yards right of the green, where it sat quietly smiling at my fuming ass as I walked up to it. Fear not fellow humans, I have better hands than Tom, so I decided to hit my low, spin lob. Me being me, I pulled off the ultimate shot. However, the ball stopped six feet above the hole. I was now faced with a down hiller with spike marks smiling at me like a Manuel Noriega face. Easy bogey, I think.

Tom looked at me after I hit the shot and said, "See, that's why it's not fair to be able to play square grooves."

I walked over to him and said, "Tom, the point your missing

is that I now have a putt that's pure luck if I make it and if I had your grooves, I would have a tap-in or 3-footer uphill. They hurt you as much as they help you, and you never know."

He looked at me with a quizzical look and said nothing. But, I could see that a light had gone off in his head and he understood that there were some disadvantages to playing square grooves. We never had another talk about square grooves again.

More time elapsed and the USGA settled the square grooves lawsuit. The PGA Tour and my buddies Deano & Timbo decided they would fight on. Then they got a wake-up call and decided to settle too. Karsten never had any intention of taking their money, he just wanted the average golfer not to have to go out and buy new irons - the exact same reason that I signed my name to the lawsuit.

I get clubs for free, the average player doesn't. Plus the damn grooves did not make the game easier. They helped you and they hurt you. Just like how we play, up and down. So let me ask you this question: Have you ever heard of two top executives costing their organization $15,000,000 and not losing their jobs? I'm going to say this and you can interpret it as you see fit: Did no one ever notice the fact that Deane Beman quit just a year after the PING settlement? Does anyone really think Beman wanted to walk away from golf? The biggest mistake was not getting that unethical soul Finchem to go with him. Think about that for a minute: Golf is the most honest sport on the planet. Tell me it's not ironic that for 40 years it was run by the two most dishonest souls in golf!

TPC CHAMPIONSHIP

The Tournament Players Championship is without a doubt the best and hardest event to win year in and year out. It's a difficult-ass course and everyone plays it. Fred Klauk, whom I mentioned as the sadist of Eagle Trace, was moved over to the TPC Stadium Course and was there most years I played there. He got the TPC greens firm as hell again. If the weather didn't help you out you had to be smart to win there, which clearly took me right out of my game. I just refused to believe you shouldn't go pin-hunting most of the time. I had some good rounds but you just can't be aggressive there, or at any of the major tracks, which might explain why I sucked at majors, too. Heaven forbid, you think I would have figured that out.

The TPC was one of the places I used to 'borrow' the range

balls, because they were brand new. When I first came on tour we had to pay to hit them! Well, a lot of my friends weren't exactly rolling in dough, so I thought the best thing to do was borrow some balls and gift them to the boys. I was a hero, I'm telling you. The Robin Hood of the PGA Tour. This routine went on for about 20-plus years, I'm glad and semi-sorry to say. I'm not going to mention my best year ever in ball acquisition, but it's very close to the distance from Danbury to Dallas.

The TPC Stadium Course is so tricky around the greens, it's scary. It doesn't get the credit for presenting the hardest up and downs from around the greens, but in my opinion it's not even close to any other tracks we play. I made a decent number of cuts, but that's only because I had a great short game. The best I ever finished was fifth in 1990 and I tell you that year I hit it so bad that I shouldn't have made the cut. The only other players who could've done what I did that week were Seve or Phil. I mean, not only did I miss 13 greens that day, but being the idiot I am, was always short-siding myself, which at the Stadium Course is a playing death sentence. I remember making bogey on 18 on Saturday, and thinking to myself, *Phew, now you don't have to play in the last group on Sunday.* Then they forecast a storm coming in and went back to threesomes so I got stuck with Calc and Jodie Mudd in the last group anyway. It was the best 75 I ever shot, period. I averaged five greens in regulation per round for the tournament and still finished fifth!

VEGAS

It was 1995 or '96 and our last event was Las Vegas. My two best buds were Calc and Greg Kraft. My second mom Dolores Cloughen, who took care of me in Florida (I stayed at her house in my school years and early pro years), was out visiting. My dad and his wife Patricia were there watching too, along with my mom and my great friend Colonel Gaddy who was caddying for me that week. We had a massive group of people and all the chaos and drama that came with it, but then the last day happened.

Krafty needed to make the cut to keep his card—he missed it by one damn shot. I played pretty badly but eagled the last hole after stinging a driver off the deck to ten feet. I was pretty studly with the driver-off-the-deck-shot, by the way. But as you can imagine, Krafty was bummed and pissed. So what's a good pal supposed to do when his best bud just lost his card and you're in Las Vegas? Well, you have a great dinner with the family and friends and then you tell them you're off to support your buddy. We then gambled until 6:15 in the morning. Yes, a mere ten hours of drinking, saying 'I'm sorry buddy I'm here for you and Sir Bud Light.'

The gambling went great and we split about $35,000 if my memory is correct. Krafty then gives me a look and says, "Hey, it's 6:15, what time do you tee off?"

"Seven-thirty!" I say loudly as I jump out of my chair and run up to the room to change clothes. I had told my gang to meet me at 6:45 since it took about 30 minutes to drive to the TPC Summerlin course. On the way downstairs I realize I can't tell my mom, dad or anyone else I've been up all night, much less that I've sucked down 30-plus beers.

There's only one round left since it was a four-day cut with no chance of making any money with one round left, so I made more money at the tables than I would have if I had shot a 62 on the final day. So thankfully I'm a good hide-my-drinking kind of guy. I show up and air-kiss all my moms, making sure I don't get too close to them, if you get my drift. I say I overslept.

We finally make it to the course where we literally walk straight to the tee. As some of you know you can do bizarre things when you've put too much beer in your belly. I birdied the first three holes and was off to the races.

Now, many of you also know that unless you keep drinking you're going to run out of gas, especially on a sunny, hot Vegas day. I was no exception. I faded, but basically made just pars and two bogeys the rest of the way. The 18 tee finally arrived. I flushed the tee shot and was left with a 185-yard 6-iron to the pin. The left side is guarded by a pond and the pin was tucked behind it. Of course I'm going for it. I make a fluid swing and completely lay the sod over the ball. I mean as fat a golf shot as any hacker would hit. Now, my six-iron flew about 180 yards back then, and I flew this shot 100 yards. It took a few bounces and disappeared into the Colonel Gaddy pond. I just laugh it off- I just want to go to bed. I walk up, guessed where the ball entered the water, and dropped a new ball. The pro I was playing with saw me and yelled over: "Wait Ken, wait! Your ball didn't go into the water, it stayed on the sprinkler head, just short of where you are now."

Now I'm perplexed. I think that because I've already dropped a ball I'm screwed and have to play the ball I just dropped. Then I turn back to see Colonel Gaddy picking up my ball. Now I'm going to get another penalty for picking up a ball in play! "Oh shit, no Colonel!" I yell. Too late.

Then Colonel attempts the vaunted stealth-ball-drop-back-in-to-the-grass-and-then-pretend-he's-looking-for-it gambit. Classic oops, what should I do? It was obvious the Golf Gods wanted me to suffer because after calling the rules officials over, it quickly becomes apparent they don't know the rule either. It took them 25 minutes to finally get the ruling and all I wanted was to go to bed, damn it.

"Give me a four shot penalty," I pleaded. I just wanted to get off the golf course. In the end I received no penalty at all. Nothing for my drop and nothing for the Gaddy pick-up-and-drop circus act.

CADDIES

One quick side note about Colonel Jack Gaddy. During my early days he caddied for me at Atlanta Country Club, which was very hilly. On the 14th hole I made the decision to putt out because the walk up to the 15th tee was a good one. I wanted to be breathing normally when I hit my next tee shot. I finished, and as I was walking off the green to start my journey, I tossed my ball to Colonel. It hit him right in the hand but unbeknownst to me the ball dropped to the ground and began rolling down this steep incline on the green.

I'm a few steps into my journey when I hear Colonel yell "GO IN!"

I look back as a stunned Kenny Knox watches my golf ball roll right past him just as he's starting his putting downstroke. The ball rolls right to the edge of the cup and stops. Why Colonel was yelling for a ball that he had failed to corral to go in the cup remains a hilarious mystery to this day, but the moral is that I missed one more putt that day.

Seeing as I'm talking about caddie gaffs, I'll tell you about Kevin "Ark" Richardson at the 1996 U.S. Open at Oakland Hills outside of Detroit. I was lucky enough to hit the very first tee shot of the tournament that year and even luckier it found the center of the fairway. We were both getting the yardage when I suddenly hear a BANG. Kevin had left the bag alone, and standing. Oops, out flew two clubs. The first slid out of the bag and just missed my ball to the left.

ABOVE: 11-year-old Ken Green in Honduras **BELOW LEFT:** Hunter Green
BELOW RIGHT: Third-place in the Disney father-child golf tournament with Hunter

LEFT: Mom at the Chrysler team Championship **ABOVE:** 1989 Ryder Cup- One of the proudest moments of my career. **BACK L to R:** Chip Beck, Tom Kite, Ken Green, Tom Watson, Mark McCumber, Curtis Strange, Lanny Wadkins, Mark O'Meara **FRONT L to R:** Fred Couples, Paul Azinger, Ray Floyd, Payne Stewart, Mark Calcavecchia **BELOW:** Sister Shelley and brother Bill

OPPOSITE TOP:
Mark Calcavecchia and
Lee Trevino at my foun-
dation tournament **OP-
POSITE BOTTOM:**
Caddie and cousin Joe
LaCava (now
Tiger's caddie) **TOP:**
Bill Poor, Don Wadkins,
Joe LaCava, Eric
Larson, Paul Azinger,
Clint Eastwood, Mark
Calcavecchia, Fred
Couples, at Pebble
Beach **BOTTOM:** Sis
Shelley

NEXT PAGE LEFT:
Shelley as the first
female Masters caddie
NEXT PAGE RIGHT:
Masters, first round
1986. Made 22-footer
for par and 300 feet of
putts in one day- best
putting round ever at
The Masters

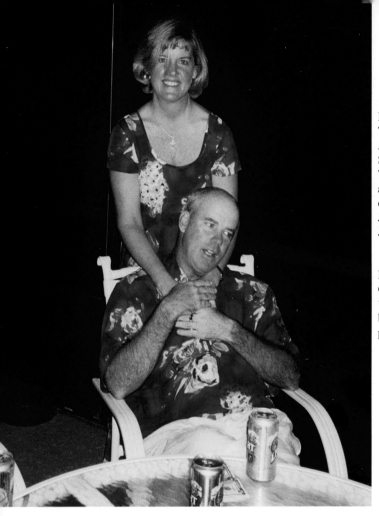

LEFT: Jeannie **BOTTOM:** Mark Calcavecchia, Atlanta Braves pitchers Steve Avery, John Smoltz, Tom Glavine, Lee Trevino at my foundation fundraiser **TOP RIGHT:** Stepson Joey, Sue, and Ken Green Jr.

BOTTOM RIGHT: Good friend Doug Ramey, 'Batman' Michael Keaton, brother and Pebble Beach pro-am partner Bill

ABOVE: 18-year-old Ken Green and the first Nip **RIGHT:** Sister Shelley

NEXT PAGE TOP LEFT: What was left of the motorhome after it crashed down a steep embankment and hit a tree, sending half of me through the front windshield leaving the other half in the vehicle **NEXT PAGE BOTTOM LEFT:** Hospital for 13 surgeries **NEXT PAGE TOP RIGHT:** Mike Reid at a Champions Tour team partner event **NEXT PAGE BOTTOM RIGHT:** Munch and I at the Senior PGA Championship, 2017

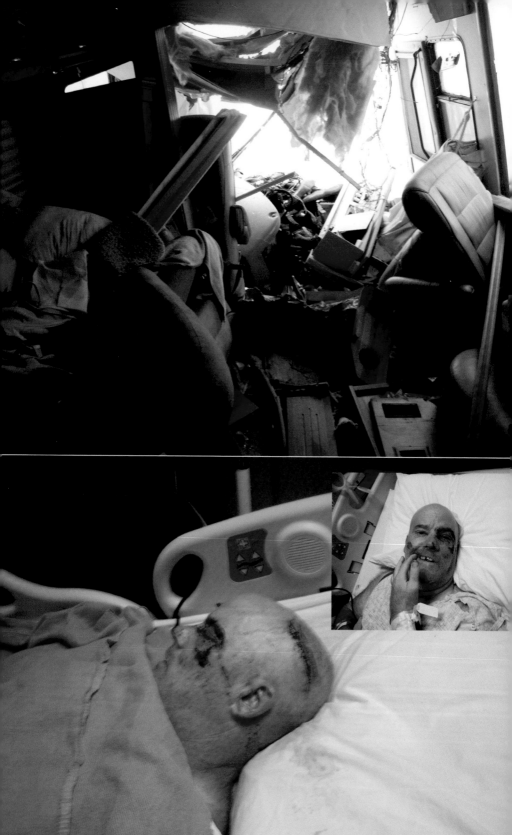

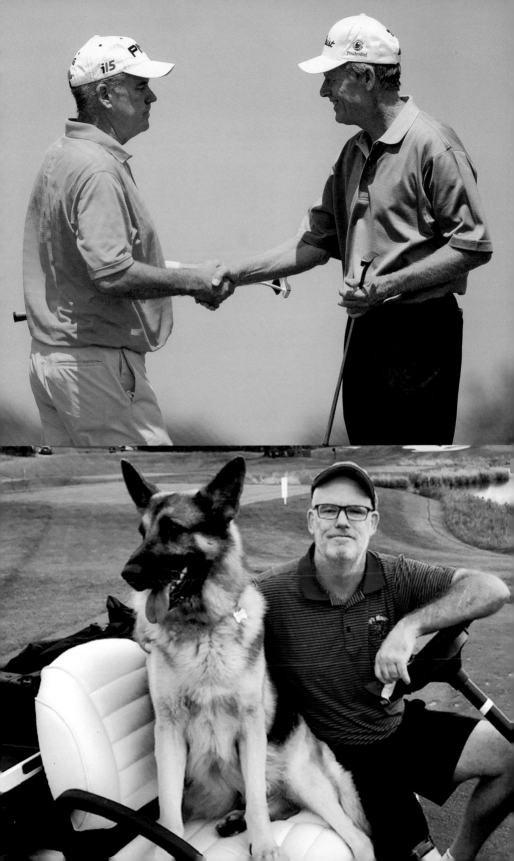

LEFT: Good buddy Major League Baseball soon-to-be Hall of Famer (!) Larry Walker **TOP:** First Tee event at Pebble Beach with playing partner Olivia Alacorn and family friend Wyatt Tournieme
BOTTOM: My girl Sue caddying for me at Pebble Beach
NEXT PAGE: The final photo of my dear son Hunter and I, December 2009

The other club missed the ball to the right- the clubs left a perfect X shape. So close to a two-shot penalty. He never left the bag standing again.

JAMS

Kapalua was where I first started wearing my brightly colored Jams pants, which were designed in Hawaii. I wore them for two main reasons. The first was that they were very colorful, but the main reason I wore them was because they were made of rayon and polyester, while all the others were cotton. I wore them because they kept you relatively cool and you didn't drip sweat all over your loved ones, caddie, local birds, etc. They also didn't show the perspiration. So I started wearing them on tour in 1992. I didn't wear them all over, but mostly in areas where it was warm as hell.

I was in contention in Memphis where it's only ninety-plus every day. I was playing with big Phil Blackmar who was soaked from his socks to the button on the top of his cap, and you could see it on TV. Meanwhile I look like I'm taking a stroll through the azaleas. Unfortunately for me that no good Jim Gallagher made a 30-footer on the last hole to keep me from a playoff. The next day I got a call from Tim Funless, Tour Commissioner. He told me my outfits were not professional looking and he was banning them from the tour. He asked why on earth I would wear those wild colors. "Tim, just look at Phil Blackmar and then look at me. It's that easy. I'm not wearing them to be a spotlight hog because I only wear them when it's hot," I said. Once again I lost that argument with my boy Tummy Finchunk. I'm now 0-8 in battles with the powers that be. My super-secret clandestine sources informed me that Davis Love III and Jeff Sluman were the instigators behind getting them banned. They didn't have the balls to come to me about it- but then again one of those two was a Yes Man who served on the PGA Tour Policy Board at the time they gave up all veto power of the players, which they'd had previously. Today all shirts are made with those materials. Mom and dad should've pumped me out 20 years later, damn it.

SOME JUDGES JUST SUCK

"Mr. Green, it's time for you to get a real job," the Connecticut judge told me during a Divorce Court session in 1984. Four years later, with a few wins on tour under my belt, I received a phone call: "Ken Green, you may not remember me but I'm the judge who told you to get a real job."

"Oh yes, what's up?" I'm kind of shocked to put it mildly.

"Well my son has joined the service and is stationed in San Diego. I'm wondering if you could leave six passes for him and some buds to go watch the PGA tournament."

I laughed and said absolutely I would. It's classic.

I had the infamous Judge Kathleen Kroll tell me she didn't care if I had to flip burgers but I needed to pay my alimony. *Right away Judge, Burger King pays their flippers $13,000 a month,* which was my monthly alimony nut. Then this judge ordered me not to have shoulder surgery because she thought I was lying in order to not pay Ellen. The Miami Heat orthopedic surgeon repaired my torn rotator cuff anyway. She said nothing upon receiving the mountains of medical work documentation that had been done on me. I should be thankful I didn't lose my leg at that point because she would've accused me of cutting my own leg off. I wasn't thinking though, I should've had my leg sent to her after it was amputated, with love of course.

In mid-2000 I had run out of money. No one knows this but I had to sell my trophy for the International that I won back in 1986. That hurt, but life is life. I also tried to sell all my PING-N-Echos that PING had gifted me. Every time a player wins a tournament with one of their putters they take that putter and gold-plate it. I cherish those puppies. But again, life is life. I called John Solheim to tell him I was hurting and asked if he could give me a value of the putters so I could try to sell them. He said, "Ken, don't do that. I'll send you something for all your support through the years. Not once did you ever leave us." I was humbled and appreciative. Two days later I received a check for $20,000. By the way, I loved old man Karsten, he was whacked but I thought he was a genius. He also was immensely loyal, which I admired greatly.

THE ASAHI CUP

The Asahi Cup was created as the first attempt at a Presidents Cup with four continents squaring off against each other. There were 12 of us on the team and on our flight over there were just ten of us in first-class- it was all ours. As you can imagine it's a long flight over so what are ten non-Mormons going to do on a 12-hour trip? Drink and play cards is absolutely right. We were having a buzzed blast for sure. Then it got heated as too much booze does to some pros. The next thing I know a two-time US Open Champ and a currently deceased Champion are screaming bloody hell at each other as the rest of us just laugh. With cat-like reflexes Payne Stewart stands up and points his finger down at the little midget. The hobbit-like guy makes a strange move and knocks down the other guy with a Payne-full bang. A stunned group of idiots looks around wondering who to wager on. One of the Marks quickly says, "A hundo on the strange hobbit character," which was followed by, "I'll take that Payne in the ass guy."

Immediately they start rolling from one end of first-class to the other with neither of them landing a blow. The match was then called by Sir Hadit from Texas. We all went to our respective seats to sleep it off. Hours pass when suddenly we're awoken by the worst turbulence known to man. We're approaching Tokyo all wondering if we're doomed. The lightning outside was so prevalent it looked like day-time. We took it like men, in complete silence except for the noisy, smelly bursts coming from parts unknown. Not one joke about the smell as we sat in fear. The silence was deafening. Mister Calc was on the other side of the plane when I decided to explain the probabilities of survival to my peers. "Calc! We're all going to fucking die!" In unison the choir let out a "Shut up Green!" I shall never forget that ride.

Oh, by the way, we won the Cup too!

15/

The Powers That Shouldn't Be

I truly believe the best way to showcase the true identity of a person is through one's actions and behavior. I will recount a few small interactions with the powers that be that are revealing of their true character.

A few months have passed since the RV accident that took the lives of my brother and wife. To many it seemed I'd lost my whole world. I was told Jack and Arnie both called me at the hospital but I was in one of my 13 surgeries. I was awake for Gary Player's call, straight from South Africa no less. We had a grand conversation I was told, but truth is I don't recall too many words. I was really pleased that they called, it clearly shows you why those three men are known as pure class. Before I ramble on about the powers that be I was also thrilled that so many of my friends came to hang with me while I played A Thousand Hallucinations during my hospital stay. My old love Sue Doceti came to see me despite massive objections from her new man. Jim Mercer and Jerry Wygant actually stayed for a week to be my "cheerleader" after sister Shell left for the birth of her first grandkid. Chris Target, brother of the evil ex Ellen, even showed up. We are still friends today, along with her sister Nancy. It's the best feeling in the world to have friends show their love for you. Well damn, there I go again, babbling on. Let's gets back to it.

It's now been a few months after the accident and I never heard from PGA Tour Commissioner Tim Finchem. I might be wrong but I doubt any other commish wouldn't have called a player if they just lost everything. So now it's six months and I get more terrible news. My boy Hunter is dead. Once again, I never heard from Tim. In my view that tells you all you need to know about the so-called leader of our tour for the past 18 years, give or take. I've made the decision to only tell a few stories of my encounters with Tim Funchump because I like to just get to the point and not flavor up my words like Shakespeare, so I'll just spit it out.

The biggest window into two men's real souls came during the infamous PING lawsuit. The idea they even had to sue was pathetic. The governing bodies didn't seem to care about the average guy who would have to trash their clubs and buy new ones if the so-called 'square grooves' were banned. Thousands and thousands of people, damn it. That being said, the two power figures would then tell lie after lie to every player and unfortunately, due to gag orders, we on the other side couldn't tell them boo. Truth be told, even if the superstars were told the real truth they wouldn't have been able to put two and two together to understand they were doomed to lose from the start, legally speaking. I love Arnie and Jack, who were against the grooves, but they didn't do their homework and they were lied to. Watson was big against it as well but I'm not a huge fan of his anyway.

The biggest common denominator among superstar golfers is ego. They are right about whatever they think they know whether they know it or not. When it came to the PING suit and the Casey Martin suit, the ego of those five men cost the tour about twenty million dollars. Now, Tom, Jack and Arnie's opinions were just that, opinions, but their words carried 90 percent of the players. The two commissioners couldn't put their ego aside, which was their job, and they subsequently fought two very bitter and unnecessary lawsuits that were both easily lost. How did it not dawn on anyone that Casey Martin's leg would only get worse and he would never keep his card for longer than maybe a year? How they both kept their jobs is beyond me. Deano conveniently left one year after the PING debacle, and it was not voluntary, if you ask me. How no one in the media put Tim + lawsuit = Lose your job, together, is amazing. How Beman didn't keep his job but Funchump did is equally bizarre. Not only did he keep his job but he gets promoted to the new Dictator Commissioner. Just shows you how we players have such tunnel vision that we're blinded sometimes.

I know I have a mini-ego and I'm very seldom wrong but I

speak only on subjects I know, where many think they know it all. I tell my friends *'I know what I know and nothing else.'* Great golfers have massive egos though. I'm just dead against our PGA Tour Commissioner and executives lying to players to further the reasoning to continue with a lawsuit in which they know they're doomed. This is what those two did best. They were bullies of the greatest order. They played rough-house with sponsors all the time. Many say that's what business is all about. I say that's why we're failing as a people. Our tour and players had no issue dumping smaller cities because those locales couldn't come up with enough cash to cover the escalating fees. Some of these had been tournaments for three or four decades and we just threw them aside like skunk piss. The GMO and BC Open for starters. Just wrong. We had to at least try and save some of these cities, I thought.

In 1983 the top-gun players were dead-set against the tour starting up the TPC golf course projects. They felt that we were golfers and should just be out there golfing. They called for a big player meeting where we were going to basically kick Dean Beman out. But Beman out-smarted the Pinkings and had printed up this beautiful booklet outlining every benefit and advantage of the PGA Tour expanding into real estate. It was brilliant. The TPC projects make the PGA Tour millions and despite my hatred of these men, it really was brilliant. I truly believe that the only reason the big-name players didn't give their blessing to the Players Championship becoming the fifth major was this loss. Jack and the gang were embarrassed and hated the fact that they got bushwhacked. How on earth could they sign off on the fifth major now? It was practically a done deal back then if you go back and look at the reporting. So how could they now give credit to Deano after that embarrassing loss. It's crazy that to this day they don't consider the Players Championship a major. It has everything a so-called Major needs, and more. Sidebar folks: I've since found out that the TPC concept was not the original idea of Beman, as he had told the world. More lies. He should be given credit for building them up, however.

I was playing in a pro-am in Vegas in the late 1990s. I'm a great pro partner if I do say so myself. I've always felt it was important to talk with the amateurs and have best time you can. Otherwise you can also just be miserable. I could take the Fuzzy Zoeller approach and yak it up or take the Curtis Strange/Greg Norman approach and don't say squat. So we're on our 50th hole and I'm missing the 54-hole cut for sure. We're at Bears Best Golf Club and the only fans out there are the family and friends of my amateurs. One of the guys brings me a beer. I know I'm not supposed to have it but I'm like *Wtf, no one is here so why not?* Oops, a tour official saw that I was drinking something so he went over to the stand and asked what was ordered. He then came over to me on the next hole and asked what I was drinking. I smiled and told him it was ginger ale, which led to a little smirk from him, so I figured we're cool. My lovable no-good brother-in-law Slugger White is Head Official, so the other official goes up to him and tells him the story and asks him what to do. Slugger tells him to report me. He later claimed he had no idea the tour would do what they did. I say bullshit you dumb shit, you know damn well Finchem hates my guts and will slam me every time he can. They've been very consistent in this matter, especially since the PING lawsuit.

So this event is the end of the year so by the time the fine arrives it's like November. A two-month suspension, my dearest Tim hits me with. Now, I'm pretty much broke. I'm doomed if I'm not allowed to play and earn some cash in January and February. Once again we go back and forth. I readily admit it was a violation but the penalty is way too severe. I'm like *Tim, we have Michelob Light plastered all over the place and yet I'm being punished for having a damn beer with the pro-am partners whom all said they were willing to tell you they bought the drink for me.* He then proceeds to tell me my history with alcohol concerned him. *Wtf are you talking about?* He then tells me how my ex accused me of being an alcoholic and he was concerned for my health. I'm lucky this wasn't a face-to-face chat or it would've been a foot-to-mouth chat. He now defends the Michelob Light by saying it's just beer. I said, "You just told me we want to protect our image so you don't allow hard alcohol, but beer is okay. I'll use that in court if I get stopped by a cop after 20 beers. 'Officer, my hero Tim Fanchunk, said beer is fine and I can drink as many as I want because it's not hard liquor.'" It's like the policy of no casino logos on any shirts, but it's okay if it says, "MGM Resorts." Total hypocrisy at its best. The bullshit selling of PR baloney. Anyway, I lost the argument that I had to play because I was dead broke and could never survive for two months without making some cash. He then says, "You're still suspended but I'll allow you to get two months of your retirement money pulled out. I said "Tim, every time I've pulled any money out

I had to show boatloads of documents from doctors explaining in full detail all my injuries. This was needed by law, I was told." He says, "Just write a letter telling them what you need. I'll okay it."

I had been forced to jump through ridiculous hoops to access *my* money in the past from the tour's pension fund. They needed reams of paperwork and crazy rationales for why I needed this money. But here was our Dear Leader who just waved his hand and could take care of it without all of the drama that had been required in the past. One more example of the truth residing nowhere near reality in the world of the PGA Tour and its compromised chieftain.

I'm not going into all the idiotic chats we had but there were too many and all of them came after the PING lawsuit where I was being punished for every single thing I could be hit up for. I got nailed by Tim for Dean losing his job. I would love to tell you more with regards to their actions in the suit but I'm sadly prohibited from doing so by court order. Clearly I don't admire or respect either one of those men. That being said I'm sure their friends and family love them and think they're good souls, and to them I'm sure they are. All I'll say is *They know I know.*

One bully-game those two pulled off was getting the players to give up their veto power. At that time the players could veto any proposal the tour made, for any reason, at any time. Somehow Beman and his legal henchman Finchem managed to convince the four dumb-shit players on the policy board that it was in their best interest if they surrendered the players' veto power. How and why they would ever agree to that is one more example of players being too tunnel-visioned to see outside their tiny cocoon. I'm guessing today's players don't even know that the players had veto power over the tour at one time. Just keep 'em all liquored up on sponsor and manufacturer cash and the dummies will do exactly what you want. I may not like the tour management cabal but they're good bullies. It's the players' tour and the players should have the final say. But they don't anymore.

16/

Nip Travels the World

In my first year in Gainesville at the University of Florida I bought a German Shepherd from a guy who lived on Newberry Road. I have also always been known to have great "hands" playing golf, meaning I could hit the short shots well; I could "nip" shots that others couldn't. Hence, I officially named my new pet Newberry Nip, or just Nip. And it was that dog's namesake, who died in the accident that took my leg and my brother and Jeannie, that is also the name for something I started casually in 1972 and have been doing to some degree every year to this day.

I honestly believe one of the reasons I have such great hands for golf is the fact that as a kid I was always outside 'playing golf' around my apartment complex in the winter with plastic balls that I taped with electric tape. I could make these balls go every which way. All through the winter and summers, when I wasn't on the golf course, I was chasing an electric-taped plastic ball around our apartment complex. It was something that I never grew out of. I and my friends would often hit shots after walking out of a bar or restaurant where we would go from door to cars to hoses to curbs to anything we saw. Remember, this was the 80s and the tight-asses weren't controlling the world just yet. The fact is, in Danbury where I lived, the cops would stroll up, look at us and just say, "Ok, don't be stupid." Fame doesn't hurt all the time.

Another game I would play on the road on tour was target

practice from my hotel room. We were playing gin after a round of golf at the Disney pro-am with some friends I had met there. We're in an intense game when we needed a break to stand up and stretch. Right outside the room, about 160 yards away, was the tent for the tenth tee at the Magnolia course. The three-sided tent was almost facing us but open more to the right side, angling towards us. Between my room and the tent however, was a big tree that blocked any type of straight shot. I then decided I was going to hit a golf ball off the bed, out an open window, and hook it about thirty yards, into the tent. I said, "Who wants 20-1 odds for a hundred that I can pull this shot off in one try?" John Evenson took the bet.

Now, I hadn't taken this into consideration but when I stood on the bed I soon found out the ceiling was much lower than I had expected. I now had to hit some sort of restricted backswing shot while following through off a porridge-soft bed where I couldn't stand still. Thank the lord I had two real legs back then. I took a few practice swings and was finally ready. I swung, I connected, it got out the window. I'd like to tell you I hooked it around the tree and turned it straight into the tent. I would. And I can, because I did do just that. One of the best fluke shots ever and two thousand dollars in my pocket.

I became so good with my hands because God gifted me with those hands (and of course lots of practice). When I was in high school and college I was constantly sneaking onto the two local area private clubs in Connecticut; Ridgewood Country Club in Danbury where I caddied often, and Morefar Golf Course, over the state line in New York. Ridgewood had a member, Bill McClauglan, who used to drive around to see if I was on the back holes where he would then report my trespassing to the pro. A few years later he became one of my sponsors and we stayed friends until his death.

Morefar was a more exclusive private club where if they got four groups a day you would consider it a traffic jam. I would often go there with Nip and just work on my short game, hitting to the different greens on the back side. The head greenskeeper hated me doing that and often chased us away, but only into the woods. He never dared follow us into the woods, probably because he just saw the movie Deliverance. One night after a session of being chased off the course I reached my car only to be greeted with a flat tire. Being the handy two-legged devil I was, I just started to change it. Suddenly a truck comes screaming up and slams on the brakes, rubber peeling. The greenskeeper jumps out and starts screaming about staying off his course. Suddenly, without warning, Nip flies out of the half-opened window and goes after him. The dude barely reached his truck before Nip got to him. Credit to him however, he was still yelling at me as the window was rolling up. Unlike old Bill, however, we never did become friends. Thirty years later and 12 global golf championships to my name, I was going to play there with a friend. When he found out I had a tee-time he called my phone and told me I'm still not allowed to play his course. The good news is my penalty was ended after 40 years, just recently. Patience is a virtue they tell me.

**

Many of the legends have agreed on one thing that's necessary to achieve success on the PGA Tour: Perseverance. Even the stud of studs only wins every so often, so how much do you think we good golfers win? Very little. So clearly you have to keep at it until you succeed.

The city of West Palm Beach has a TGIFriday's only a mile from Bear Lakes Country Club where I played for five years or so. My friends and I would gather after a round of golf, and after we had drowned our sorrows (or whatever we were drinking for that day) we would head out to the parking lot to attempt a shot-of-shots.

We all knew to park in a secluded part of the parking lot in anticipation of our post-bevy competition. About 160 yards away from where we all parked our cars there was the infamous Prudential building. On the top of that building, which was quite high, was the Prudential rock logo sign. It was this recognizable symbol that we spent years trying to hit. *Years, damn it.* Then finally I managed to hit a rocket-high shot that hooked right into the middle of 'The Rock.' Luckily for me my buddy Mike Farmer was there to witness the amazing feat. From that point on we never tried again because once you achieve your goal you move on to another, don't you?

That said, every time we left the restaurant we would all look up and see this big blue The Rock sign shimmering blue, except for a little dot of white light that shone through from the bullet I had shot through the dragon's heart. Then one day we looked up and low and behold they had fixed The Rock! The cheapos just put a patch of blue paint over the hole. Now there was the dim blue hue with a bright blue hue where my ball mark was repaired. At least they repair their ball marks at The Rock.

**

It was a gorgeous night in Hawaii and I'm staying at the top floor in a relatively tall hotel overlooking the main drag and also the infamous Waikiki beach. The room is a corner room so I have two porches. One faces Waikiki and the other faces a hotel about 150 yards out. The other hotel is not as high as ours and it has a pool on top of their roof. It's beautiful; the lit pool mixed with other lights scattered about on the rooftop. After about my 10th ball into the ocean-side a light bulb went off and I decided to see if I could hit it out the window, over the railing and into the pool on top of the hotel across from me, about an 8-iron away. This was a no brainer—I would clearly be able to see the balls splash into the pool. Once again I'd like to say I got it in on my first try. This time however, I can't tell you this. I hit all 30 balls I had out my window and not only did I not get the first one in, I never got any of them in! But I had a blast trying. I borrowed another bag from the range the following day and yes, this time I was a miserable failure again. I still haven't figured out why that shot was so hard. Was there some cosmic wind howling outside that I couldn't see? I'll never know.

The Nip Open courses are quite different in Japan. Over there tall buildings are commonplace. One has to be creative as all hell to devise a shot out of the rooms there. The good news is that I'm mentally deranged so it didn't take long. On the other side of the boulevard was another hotel across from mine. The boulevard had three lanes on each side so I was guessing from my room to the hotel was about an 80-90 yard shot. I did reconnaissance the first night. The second night I decided what my target would be: a porch on the adjacent hotel that was a couple floors below me and a shade to the left, which made my angle of attack a tad easier (if you haven't figured this out yet, I take my trick shots seriously). My target was a chair on that porch- I was going to try and see if I could keep the ball on the porch. That would be a hole-in-porch, but a great shot would just hit the porch and have the ball fall off. Truthfully, I was a little scared because this was not the most appropriate thing to do. But I had to hit a few Nips in Tokyo, I told myself. It's now late and the roads are basically empty and I'm pretty sure I'm good to go. I decided I was only going to hit three shots. The first left the room on a perfect trajectory. I rushed out of the room to see if I hit my target. I didn't account for my adrenaline and was two floors too high, but I did hit the porch railing. The ball then fell straight down and hit the concrete, bouncing back up quite high. It bounced so many times people started to notice- I watched from the shadows as people looked around trying to spot the idiot dropping golf balls from on high. I was smirking and scared at the same time. I didn't have the cojones to hit shot two or three.

I eventually turned my one man Nips into a Nip Open tournament where we pick out targets around my property in Florida- car tires, tree trunks, bird baths, bottles, beer cans, etc. We hit balls over my house, through my house, through my RV, and all around the property. Sometimes windows get busted, sometimes they don't, but one thing is certain, only the best of people get invited to the Nip of Nips.

17/

Why One Falls

So how do I explain the multi-year stretch where I finally collapse into a deep state of depression? Before I get too far into it I should state that I don't want anyone to think I am laying the blame for depression on anyone other than Mr. Ken Green. I'm the one responsible for not being able to reproduce serotonin and falling into a suicidal state. I'm the idiot who, at the urging of my ex-wife Ellen, pushed my mom, sis, brother and some friends away. When I look back at some of these stories I actually laugh and wonder how I could have been so dumb. But it was Ken Green making the final call in all of this. I guess the love bug just turns your brain into crushed marbles sometimes.

You've read some stories about my descent into the depression rabbit-hole, but these explain even more why I fell apart. They are all just factual stories of what I went through in this Green odyssey.

First off, during my divorce case with Ellen, we set a record at the time for the most pleadings in a divorce case in the state of Florida. A mere 1600 pleadings! I'm not sure if this is a record I still own but I have to believe I'm near the top. Take a second and grasp that—*it's insane.*

At one point I had a judge tell me she didn't care how I paid the $13,000 alimony a month. "Go flip burgers if you have to, or go find a real job," is literally what she told me in court. How she's a judge is beyond me. This same judge who I had for the first six years of court made me pay for all court costs and attorney's fees Ellen incurred with each of her 11 different lawyers. Funny how the litany of pleadings ended when we got a different judge who ordered her to pay her own legal fees.

When we finally decided to go through with the divorce I didn't see my three kids, Brad, Brooke, and Hunter, for six months. I had tried to adopt Brad and Brooke but their father refused. Hunter was our biological son. I wouldn't see Hunter because I kept trying to convince Ellen to let me see all the kids at the same time. I had been their dad for six years damn it and loved them like I did Hunter and Ken Jr. Ellen was stronger than the Hoover Damn though and never budged. I finally had no choice but to just see Hunter alone.

Ellen demanded I not be allowed into the Steeplechase home, which we had shared and I had given her in the divorce, and as such I had been mandated to pick up Hunter at the guard gate out front of the development. Hunter got in the car eagerly (this was before the corruption would begin). I'll never ever forget his first words to me: "Why aren't Brad and Brooke coming and why are you picking me up out here?" These words haunt me today. For the next seven years it was court after court after court. She did everything in her power to keep me from seeing my boy and while doing that she crushed us both. She wanted to do damage to me but in the process she affected both of us, and one of us was a child. She had no clue the damage she was doing to Hunter. Sadly we would find out January 22, 2010 when Hunter would die of a drug overdose while at college at Southern Methodist University.

The 1600 pleadings should tell you plenty. I was brought into court because I let Hunter play in dirt piles with his friends. I was pulled into court for bringing Hunter to a bowling alley. Ellen and the kids were shown on video keying my vehicles a couple of times. Ellen was seen going through our garbage and was given a pass by the judge in the case because she claimed, "It was a unique way of discovery." She and Sheryl Calcavecchia were caught hiding outside our yard listening to our conversations. One night they showed up, their faces pressed against the glass of my sliding door on the porch, listening for God knows what.

Ellen often showed up with another friend with the police in tow to check on Hunter's wellbeing, telling the police he was in danger. When the police entered they would always find a laughing, playing Hunter, just a regular kid. She accused my friend and Connecticut lawyer of pushing her out the door and to the ground, and it made all the Danbury papers. One summer night in my Danbury condo she tried to break into the condo via the kitchen window. She was trying to get Hunter three weeks before his summer was over with me. Fred's wife at the time, Deborah Couples, was with her that night and they zoomed off after we woke up hearing the glass break. The police couldn't do anything as all we had as evidence was footprints and a few bracelets that broke off as she tried to climb in. Deborah called me a couple years later and apologized for letting Ellen convince her to help her. The very next day Ellen came to the condo and grabbed Hunter away from us. Sue, my partner at the time and the love of my life ever since, was home but elected not to fight with Ellen as it would be way too stressful for the kids. Ellen stole my car from the lot once when she was in Connecticut.

One day Sue and I went to pick up Hunter from a travel hockey trip when the team got back. Everyone was just hanging around and the kids were doing kid things like running and playing. We then watch Ellen go into a frenzy, "Where is Hunter, where is Hunter?" Sue watched as Brad and Brooke, on Ellen's orders, slid Hunter into a big hockey bag and strolled toward the car, basically a self-imposed kidnapping. I swear to god you can't make this stuff up.

I'm not going into all the police reports and times they were brought into all the child pick-ups and other issues. She would file and have arrest warrants issued as soon as she could and I remember once after I got screwed out of another weekend we were able to get into court that same night. We had a temporary judge and not the crazy Ellen-lover Judge Kathleen Kroll. After testifying, the judge ordered Ellen to jail for the weekend. I remember telling my attorney Kevin that this wasn't what I wanted. I only wanted to see Hunter and stop all this nonsense. Kevin spoke up and told the Judge I didn't want Ellen in jail, I just wanted to see my son. The Judge said fine and then told Ellen to write a sentence two hundred times and show it to Judge Kroll. "I will never interfere with visitation again and I will let my son see his dad," she had to write, like a child. One might think she would've learned but I would soon have another arrest warrant out on me. But it all came to a head when she accused me of assault.

The local prosecutor wanted to create a name for himself so

he took the case and in 1995 I was charged with assault. This, despite Ellen's affidavit changing FOUR times. Mine never changed. As predicted it was picked up by the media and of course everyone just assumed a hot-head on the course would be a hot-head at home. My lawyer suggested I accept the plea offer. I said no way. I wasn't going to plead to something I was innocent of. We elected to go for a bench (judge's) trial instead of a jury trial since I figured the odds of getting three straight idiot judges was slim. Ellen showed up and amazingly even brought the kids to the bogus trial. The Judge ordered them out immediately when he was told who they were. She testified and then had to leave the court also. They waited outside. I testified, and after hearing both stories the Judge ruled immediately- in my favor. He was adamant in his verbal ruling and his Judgment of Acquittal that it was clear Ellen was a lady who was out for blood and was completely lying. My mother was at the trial and when he ruled she burst into uncontrollable tears and had to be helped out by Sue and another friend. Literally right outside the door was Ellen and the kids sitting on a bench. When Ellen saw her crying so hard she assumed she had won. She was overheard telling the kids that daddy hurt mommy badly and had to pay!

I'm hoping at this point you might start to understand why I fell into depression. At some point your body stops producing serotonin, which is the reason people fall into depression. What I had to do next was even more difficult.

When it was clear to me that she had won by destroying my sanity and Hunter and his soul, I finally succumbed and told Hunter that I would not be able to see him for a while, but that when things got better, and he's ready to see me, that he will know where to find me. He was about 11 at this time and it broke my heart.

It was four long years before Hunter and I started seeing each other again. I stayed in touch only through phone calls. I remember thinking that if I knew she was going to torch the kids like this I would've stayed in the marriage until the kids were of college age. I never, ever dreamed she would do this to our three kids. Never. Ellen's ex was a carpenter and not making whole lot of money so I told Ellen to tell him to stop paying child support- we had plenty and he didn't, simple as that. So she did and he stopped paying.

Right after our divorce ended Ellen went to the Connecticut courts and filed for back child support saying her ex stopped paying—

because she told him to! I actually testified for him in court saying just that, but the courts said that's meaningless and they threw the book at him, thanks to her. That's Ellen.

You might be wondering why I fell in love with a lady like Ellen, and I do ask myself that, but she did have a really nice side and I got sucked in, I guess. I don't know. I've never been good with women or relationships—probably stems from my experiences as a child. There is zero doubt in my mind that if Ellen had not hated Ken Green with such a passion, Hunter would be alive today.

The last thing I will tell you is this, and this alone will tell you what kind of sad soul I was dealing with in Ellen:

My friend Guy Kennen worked with Ellen's son Brad at John Deere. Guy calls me one night and asks if Hunter is okay. I said "Yes, as far as I know, I just talked to him last night." He was concerned because Brad had asked him for my telephone number, which made no sense to either one of us. I sent a text to Hunter but he didn't reply, which wasn't a big deal because he would take a minute or a day to get back to me. Hunter and I had finally repaired our relationship a few years prior and he was spending many days with me in the RV where I was living on the Arrigo Dodge lot in West Palm Beach. Hunter and Ellen fought all the time so he would rather hang with me in the luxurious feral-cat haven RV than with her.

So the next day Guy calls me and says Brad took a few days off. He also told me that Brad's boss yelled at Guy for trying to get to the bottom of what was happening with Hunter, with Brad. The no-good scumbag knew what happened to my son and he told Guy not to worry, all was good. So when Guy told me that, and Hunter still hadn't responded, I started calling Ellen and of course she refused to answer. I was then starting to worry and wonder what the hell was going on.

I then got a call from my pain doctor who left a message saying he was sorry to hear about Hunter and that everything would be all right. Now I'm thinking he was in some sort of accident. I tried calling the doctor back but couldn't get an answer. I left a message asking him to call me. I told him I couldn't get ahold of Hunter and that Ellen was refusing to answer any calls. So after some thought I called my good friend and lawyer Kevin Richardson. I started filling him in and asked him how I would go about calling hospitals since it was my understanding he might have been in some type of accident. When I stopped talking there was a long pause and then Kevin said,

"Ken, your son is dead."

I sat there alone and stunned. Six months after you lose your wife and brother along with your leg, your boy is gone. I was crushed.

When my pain doctor realized that I had not been told he had called Kevin, whom he knew. The doctor just didn't have the heart to tell me. So the next day I'm trying to figure things out. I try calling Ellen with zero response again. My niece Nicole actually tracked down the funeral home in Dallas where his body was, since he was there attending Southern Methodist University. I called them and informed them who I was. They said that there must have been a mistake, and that Hunter Green's dad was in fact, dead.

Ellen had told the funeral home that my son's dad was dead.

I then had to send proof of who I was to the funeral home. Soon thereafter I received a call from Brooke and I asked her where they were going to bury Hunter and where the services were going to be. I knew I wouldn't attend because I knew Ellen would turn our child's death into a melodrama about her. I just wanted to know where he was going to be buried so I could pay my respects and love. Then Ellen got on the phone and started screaming that Hunter was hers and that I will never have him. She then screamed about him being cremated. I then asked if she would save some of his ashes for me to lay with Jeannie, Billy and my father and mother. She screamed "Never!" and hung up.

I was stuck wondering how 17 years later she still had all this venom. Our boy, whom we created with our love, was dead, damn it. *What the fuck is the matter with you?*

That night, without my consent (which in Texas you can do) she moved Hunter's remains to another funeral home and then immediately sent him off to New Mexico where he was buried. How do you respond to that when you find all this out? She buried our boy in some random graveyard in New Mexico, some place no one in our family had ever even been! Ellen had no intention of ever telling Hunter's father that he was dead, much less any information about his burial.

I'm haunted by not making a decision, with Sue's blessing, many years earlier. When the debacle with Ellen was gaining steam and both Sue and I could see the damage she was doing to Hunter, we had planned, and I mean we had made most of the arrangements, to disappear with Joey (Sue's child, over whom she had sole custody) and Hunter. I was going to leave golf and we were going to take the kids and run to New Zealand or as far away as we could go. We were watching a young boy being destroyed by his parents' animosity. I will take a tenth of the blame because I should've known Ellen wasn't going to stop until I was destroyed, and in the process she had destroyed our boy.

But I didn't. And now all that regret came flooding back over me. Fucking New Mexico? What the fuck is wrong with her? My boy is in New Mexico, damn it. We're Florida and Connecticut people. I'm guessing by now she has moved him, but I honestly have no idea.

I still blame only myself for falling into depression but I'm guessing you might understand why I fell into that hole, knowing just this story alone. Just imagine fighting through this for seven years and the damage done to all three kids, not to mention to me. I loved this lady. How the hell did this all happen?

Depression is a vicious disease simply because you never feel like you're sick. It's one of the hardest diseases to detect. That's why so many souls literally live their lives in a state of depression and don't even know it.

18/

Suicide

There's a three-year period of my life where you could have convinced me I visited the Pyramids, slept with Demi Moore, and won the Puerto Rican lottery. I would have had to believe you because I had no memory of those years, that's how severe my depression was. The period from 1998 to 2000 was a mystery world. I have practically no recollection of those years. After seven-plus years of divorce and custody court, fighting for my son, I had to let my boy go. Hunter's mom Ellen was destroying the boy and he didn't know it. The hardest choice I have ever made in my life (way more difficult than telling the doctors to cut off my leg) was telling Hunter he was free not to visit or see me. Ellen had won the battle but with all the fighting she had damaged Hunter and she had damaged me. Eventually that damage led to us all losing the war.

Recounting this part of my life is extremely difficult. Bringing back memories of Hunter is harder than I realized. I had no idea when or even if Hunter would come back to me. I was in full bore depression and had no clue what was going on around me. And keep in mind I was playing professional golf at the highest level in the world. I look back on the evolution of my suicide attempt and realize it took me a little more time to reach the point of saying adios. I've learned we all have various reasons why we lose the serotonin in our brain. Without wanting to I was about to become my father and abandon my son— certainly for different reasons but the same damn results. I had worked hard at my profession and had amassed a few million dollars, only to watch it all disappear through my divorce with Ellen. Half of it went to her, another $200,000 to her eleven (*yes*, 11) lawyers, plus some of my assets from before we were married were given to her by the less than honorable Judge Broom because she claimed I intended to give those assets to her at some point in the future.

I was now out of control with my personal life- I was drinking too much and making my dream girl's life hard. I finally lost my exempt status on the PGA Tour and had no idea what or how I was going to get through this period of darkness. I vaguely remember Sue telling me she thought I was in a state of depression but of course me being the stubborn-ass mule that I am, I refused to even entertain that possibility. I really had no clue what depression was much less what it does to you or how to fix it.

I've since learned that there are two distinct kinds of depression, one where you actually just live out your life as a miserable soul, never really knowing or believing you're in an altered state, and the second is the one that takes tens of thousands of lives every year; those who are strong enough to actually take their life. Those who don't understand depression think that you're a coward if you take your life. What they don't understand is that you are literally not you. You think completely differently than you used to. In my case I just kept telling myself what I've always said to myself: Suck it up nitwit 'cause life is hard and you've just got to fight through it. So here I am thinking I'm going to just keep fighting through it. The shock and loss of losing the visitations with my youngest son was the final straw.

On my way home from playing golf on a Monday afternoon I stopped at a TGI Fridays for a few drinks. By the time I left at 9:40pm I knew I was going to call it quits. I'm hoping you will see how a depressed soul sees things. In my view there was no doubt that everyone around me would be in better shape if I was gone. I figured Hunter would calm down and get over his loss soon enough. I knew Sue would be better off because I was a shell of the man I used to be. My friends would get over it and tell great stories of their legendary nut-job friend. It was about the easiest decision I had ever made in my life.

When I walked into the house the TV was on and Sue was asleep on the couch. I turned the television off as our dogs Blackie, Coco, Colonel, and Casper welcomed me with their usual wagging tails and kisses. I tried to wake Sue up—I even asked her to have sex with me, for what I knew was one last time. She opened her eyes, smiled wanly and said, "Go to bed asshole." That was her 'fun' nickname for me- she still uses it to this day.

I smiled and nodded, then went into the bathroom without hesitation. I opened a bottle of sleeping pills, a bottle of pain pills and a bottle of Advil. I looked at the collected 100-plus multicolored pills and thought that if this didn't kill me I probably had a career as a superhero. I was sure I had enough to ensure I would leave this world behind forever.

I popped the pills in my mouth in 30-pill increments and washed them down with a beer. The rest of this story comes from Sue.

She says that Coco, our golden lab, kept nudging at her on the couch. The dog pushed her face under Sue's arm and nudged and jabbed at her. Sue kept pushing her away and told her to go lie down. Thankfully Coco was as stubborn as her daddy because she wouldn't give up. Finally, Coco put her mouth on a sleeping Sue's arm and literally yanked her off the couch. Sue woke up yelling at Coco.

"Coco you damn mutt!" she said as she chased the dog toward the bedroom, all the while giving her a piece of her mind. When she finally turned the corner and came into the bedroom Coco jumped up on the bed and was lying right on top of me as I slept, drifting away to leave what I believed was a better world for those left behind.

When Sue saw this bizarre scene on the bed she realized something was very, very wrong. She rushed over and saw I was still breathing. She saw the pill bottles in the bathroom and called the ambulance. I woke up in the hospital three days later, thanks to angels named Sue Doceti and Coco the dog. And in her infinite wisdom Sue had even registered me as "Kenneth Flowers," knowing that if it got out that Ken Green had tried to kill himself it would have been a media frenzy.

So "Kenneth Flowers" spent the following 72-hours in West Palm Beach's mental ward. It was there that I realized how many people are hurting in our society. It was then that I realized perhaps my issues weren't the life-ending ones I had imagined them to be. But I wasn't out of the woods yet.

19/

Recovering from Depression

I can promise you that if you've never suffered from depression you may not fathom what I'm going to say: I would rather have cancer or heart issues than suffer through depression.

I mean nothing against those who have fought those ugly diseases, but the key is you knew your life was at risk. You knew you had a problem. Then you made corresponding decisions with a team at your side; physicians, family, friends, and technology. You fought the best you could and will either win or lose. I have no recollection of my life between 1998 and 2000, or if I do they are just glimpses of my life. How's that harder to fight, you wonder? Well, first I have no idea I'm not normal because I would bet my life I was rational and completely put together. So I'm putting my life in jeopardy by doing stupid ass things, but worse, I put Sue and Joey's lives in danger too. Yet I refused to even entertain the thought I was not me. My last straw, where I went deep into the ugly-hole, was when I let Hunter go, never knowing if I would get him back. After Sue left I was not even close to pulling myself out of the depression. I was on pills but it often takes time to find the right pill that works for you and then the right dosage.

Near the end of 2001 I was starting to feel like myself again. My issues were all still there but how I saw them and handled them was the way the "normal" Ken Green would've recognized and handled them. How a pill convinces the brain to produce more serotonin is beyond my pay grade but it does and it did. Everything still sucked

(I had no status on tour, no girl, no cash, and I'm old in tour years) but no one was in danger and I was ready to take on the world all over again. The question was how the hell would I do this? I'm 43-years-old with zero cash.

The Q school was out in Palm Springs in the winter of 2002 so I went out there with Jeannie and good friend Craig Thomas who was a golf pro and a longtime friend who caddied for me. It was a six-round beast of a week where two swings could cost you a year. It was, and still remains to this day, the ultimate pressure cooker in golf.

Going into the last day I wasn't even close to the top. I was in the middle but knew if I played a good round I could jump into the top fifty due to pressure the others would feel and the fact that the better golfers near the top were all on the hard course that I had spent my earlier three rounds on. Now, I was fighting a spasmodic back all week, but you just pray you don't get a spasm right in the middle of your swing.

I played a great round on the last day and made it. Ken Green was heading back to the tour. *Wow* I couldn't believe it. I was so ready to get out there and prove to myself I could come back from this holy hell I was in.

The money was getting crazy at that point. I got $300,000 just for agreeing to use a driver for the year. I got another $70,000 for a bunch of other equipment. It was insane to me but I was broke and for the first time in years I was not going to have to worry about money. Imagine that; no money worries while I played golf. I can honestly tell you I never once choked under the pressure while trying to win a golf tournament, not once. I will also tell you that I choked all the time when money was an issue or I had an arrest warrant out for me. If I was finishing thirtieth place I blew it on the last couple holes and finished fortieth and cost myself much needed cash. You can't play golf thinking about money, kids, court—with depression to boot.

The new year started out pretty great. In my previous stint on tour, even when I was good, the West Coast swing was always terrible for me. Every year. This time out I had two of my better finishes at Pebble Beach and San Diego, making about $80,000 or so in those two tourneys. Things were going well. And we hadn't even hit the summer yet where I typically killed it. I was psyched.

Then my back went out. Pure spasms that would drop me to my knees. After missing the cut in a Florida event with a spasmodic back, I made the choice to take medical relief and rest to try and fix the issue that no one seemed to be able to diagnose, much less fix. How rare it was for me to be smart and cautious. After one full year off we still hadn't figured out why or what was causing the spasms in my back. The only thing we knew was that walking triggered it the most, which obviously does me no good when playing on the PGA Tour. Then I reverted back to the old Ken Green and decided to play through the pain for the rest of 2004. Big mistake. I lost my card again.

20/

Accident

We were driving back home to Jeannie's house in Greensboro after finishing a crucial four-week stretch of Alabama, Ohio, Iowa and Texas, all traveled in my Holiday Rambler motor home. I had asked my brother Bill to caddie for two weeks to see if he would eventually take it on regularly, and Jeannie was on a rare trip on tour. This was our mulligan on life so I had to make sure we made enough money to keep us afloat for our end-days. The first two weeks went by great. Billy and Jeannie were fantastic and we had a blast together, on and off the course. The golf was just fair and I finished in the middle of the pack. Iowa was the third event and I played a bit better.

Our last journey was to Austin, Texas. I once again had a decent finish and we were off to North Carolina. I decided we would drive to Shreveport and park in the lot of a casino I know there. The next day we took off about noon for our ten-hour drive. I was the night driver due to Bill's poor eyesight at night so I decided to go take a nap in the back bed while he chewed up the daylight hours. Before I went back I told them both this:

"From here on in we're as good as gold and we are going to make a fortune."

They both looked at me with blank stares. I clarified, "What I mean is that even though I didn't finish top ten or win I know we're going to when my game turns around because I haven't told you, but I just played two straight weeks without one demon in my head or one demon interfering with a shot. I'm back to being Ken Green and I'm going to destroy them. Goodnight." Those are literally the last words my brother and wife ever heard me say.

I am dreaming like a puppy dog without a worry in the world when all of a sudden a loud bang wakes me straight up. From there onward is pure speculation. Based on the position of the RV, and me, at the time of the crash, it was assumed that I had heard the tire blow, woke up, and ran forward to see what was going on. I must have almost reached Billy and Jeannie in the front when we crashed into a tree and I flew out the front window. Three quarters of me was found outside the window with one side of my right leg outside and the other side inside, slashed to pieces- practically cut in two. Billy, Jeannie and Nip were killed instantly. I lay in nasty Mississippi swamp water for who knows how long until they managed to pull me out of there. I was air-lifted to the Jackson Memorial Hospital where I woke up a day or so later.

I woke up to see my sister Shelley holding my hand. "Hey sis what are you doing here?" Like I even knew where I was. "Sis what's going on?" She looks at me with tears falling from her eyes.

"Green, you guys were in an accident. The front tire blew and you guys went straight into a big tree."

"Wow," I said. "How is everyone else doing?"

The tears are coming faster now, and I start to cry.

"How bad?"

"Ken, they're all dead."

We were all just crying now. My three closest family members were all gone. My wife, my brother and my precious Nip, gone.

We eventually stopped crying when I asked what was wrong with me and told her it really hurt. Then the doctor and Shelley and other family members came in to talk to me. I felt like I was about to talk to the principal.

I wasn't aware of this but the doctors had told them that they should cut the leg off. They didn't believe I would allow that because golf was everything to me. The doctor then went through his spiel and basically told me that if we kept the leg I would never have close to full strength and would be dragging it all around while I walked. I then said, "So you mean I can't ever really put any pressure on the leg?" He said no. I said, "Cut it off now. I'll figure out how to play golf with a piece of metal. I can't figure out how to play golf when I can't put any pressure on my leg and will be just dragging the damn thing around."

My sister Shelley told me I had damage in my eye and a huge hole in my head plus the damage to my leg. "They've pieced you together as well as they can for now," she explained through the tears.

For the next couple of days we just hung out and cried while waiting to see what to do with my defective body parts. A few more days later and, as I've outlined, I asked them to remove my leg. The resulting pain was intense. My head was throbbing with the power of three migraines and my leg was insane with pain. Whatever drugs they were giving me were not working.

I complained like a mad dog and they finally decided to up the morphine and that night I had a wild reaction to the drug. I pulled out my catheter and took off all the bandages on my head. Then I evidently decided to take a walk. I simply got, up took a step, followed by another, which for some reason didn't hit the floor. *Down goes Greenie!* The yell of pained stupidity woke Shelley up immediately. She comes over and helps me back into bed while she screams for the nurses. I'm like "Shit sis, wtf happened?"

"Greenie, don't you remember? You guys were in an accident and they all died. You also lost your leg."

"Bullshit Shell my leg is right there damn it."

"No it's not Greenie."

"Shell, have you lost your marbles, I'm fine."

This went on until they rebandaged me and stuck that stupid-ass catheter back in me and gave me enough juice to zone me. They then switched from morphine to another pain medication to keep me from running up my hospital tab pulling out catheters and ripping off perfectly good bandages.

I then started thinking that no one would be dead if I hadn't asked them to do another couple of weeks because the first two went so well. I remember thinking that I knew I had no control over this nightmare but they were my responsibility- mine alone. This will always be with me. I know it was an accident, a terrible tragedy, but I feel responsible. It helps thinking that only the Big Guy decides when we go home.

So I now start to refocus my head into getting healthy and regrouping. The pain was like nothing I had ever endured, and I've had a lot of pain.

My leg was on fire. The stupid 15-minute morphine drip was bullshit. The hospital protocols are insane. Easy enough for them to tell you to wait and hang in there. I told the doctor to keep upping the dose or I'll stick a shotgun up his ass. That didn't work either. I'm stuck in Jackson, Mississippi, after being air-lifted there from mile marker 118 on I-26. Surely I could find a fucking shotgun in Mississippi.

"So let me get this straight Shell. I lost Jeannie, Billy, Nip, my leg, and my career?"

Ooof.

21/

Jeannie My Love

Unlike most pros of any generation, I actually talked to my pro-am partners. If I didn't I never would have met Jeannie.

In 1984 I played in the Greensboro pro-am where I met this good-natured Carolinian fat-belly lefty golfer that I would eventually love to death. Norm Hodgin was his name. His wife, and my soon-to-be second Mom, Libby, was also watching. We had a good time, but that week ended and off I went.

The very next year Libby was out watching me again and that week we started a true friendship that would last until today, though all have now passed on. Before I knew it I was having dinner at their home along with their band of grown kids. I was floored at how close they were to their kids and grandkids. It was the perfect image of what you would want with all your kids. Now, Norm must've been a horny dude because he had six kids; Rick, Andy, Steve, Nancy, Ann and Jeannie. The next couple of years I would stay with Norm and Libby during tournament week. We had a blast, we played wiffleball and all sorts of games with everyone. Even Libby would swing and run around the bases. It just made that week feel like you're just there having fun- maybe that's why I played so well at Forest Oaks Country Club. Jeannie and her then-husband would drive up from Charlotte during the week. Every time I saw her she was the happiest smiling face I had ever known. She just radiated happiness. I always admired that in her.

Fast forward to the year 2000 and I was once again playing in Greensboro, staying with Libby as Norm had passed a couple of years earlier. That week I met Jeannie again and for the first time since we met we were both single. We connected immediately and from there on it was just *Boom!* I finally got to be with that radiant lady of joy. The opinions I had formed of Jeannie over the years all turned out to be spot on; she was that happy, laughing, radiant lady. She even laughed at my whacked-out sense of humor. Within six months I offered her my twenty-question Bulletin on Love. If she said yes to 18 of them, she was a keeper. She hit the bullseye with all twenty! She moved in with me right after that. We would be married a few years later on a cruise ship in the Bahamas. We knew it wasn't legally binding in the USA but it was for us and that's all we needed.

Jeannie was new to the golf world and she sacrificed for her new love. She was great to travel with while I was desperately trying to regain my playing privileges on the PGA Tour. She would even learn to caddy so we could save a few bucks at the beginning. It was a great week when in the Fall of 2002 I had re-qualified for the tour at the Palm Springs Q School. I was fully out of my depression and ready to try the tour again at the ripe old age of forty-two. Peter Kostis has said that getting my card back after all I had been through, and at my age, was one of the most impressive sporting feats he's ever seen.

Unfortunately, things don't always work out the way you hope. After my best start ever on the West Coast my back blew up and after two months my chances of tour golf were put on hold until we could resolve the back issues. The next few years were very tough as I was not pleased that my back was causing my chance at redemption to sputter and fail.

Jeannie was always there for me and never wavered. When the prognosis was "No golf, period," I made the decision that now at age forty-five I would just wait until I turned fifty where I would have another shot at redemption, this time on the Champions Tour. Jeannie and I just basically hung out and waited as patiently as we could for the Champions Tour. The great thing about Jeannie was that she was as laid back as I was, so even though we spent a lot of time together we never fought, ever.

There is not a day that goes by that I don't think of Baby.

22/

Some Doctors Just Suck

I 'd like to explain what hardcore pain is but I'm not sure I will ever be able to explain it properly. After my thirteenth surgery and seven weeks in the hospital, I was free to fly the hell out of the hospital and into a private plane the tour paid for to ship me back to sister Shelley's house. I was about to kick them out of their downstairs master bedroom. My theory was that it was about time Slugger White, my brother-in-law tour official, got boned after the three times he hosed me out there on tour. One would think you might get some love from your in-law, but not sticky old West Virginian Sluggo.

I'm told by my doctor at the time, and my prosthetics guy, that I will have pretty bad pain for a couple years. I tried to explain very clearly that it seemed like the pain I'm feeling is worse than pain, but I kept getting the *This is normal just suck it up*, reply. I'm like *Are you really telling me that each amputee goes through this intense electric bolt constant pain?* I'm getting shocks of electric-feeling bolts all day long. Sometimes they're just wowsy and other times I'm knocked off my feet. All day long. Many of you may have experienced sciatica bolts- that's exactly what it feels like. I just tell myself that I will suck it up and not complain because everyone keeps telling me it will be like this for two years. *Holy shit, I'm a weenie, damn it.* Damn pissed off weenie, I might add. So I just keep trying to suck it up and not bitch. It's getting harder and harder as time goes on. During this two year "waiting period" I come up with the conclusion that certain things I do make the leg go into Get Me Off This Planet moments. I realize that God has a classic personality, he won't let me drown my sorrows with alcohol as each time I drink, my leg goes into orbit. So I stopped drinking without an issue because I want nothing to do with bolt-Ken-bolt. I can't fly. I can't go into loud restaurants or movie theaters. I guess the vibration sets the nerves off, but that's my diagnosis, which is better than any doctor I've seen so far. Storms rip me apart. An intense storm came in out of nowhere and lightning hit as I was walking in the house. I got thrown down to the ground like a twig. It stormed for over an hour. I laid on the floor for two hours twitching like I'm having seizures or something. My three German Shepherd's-Dream, Knight and Munch, all laid on me and didn't move until it stopped. Never once did they get off me and I'll never forget the love they had for me. Dogs are amazing.

Electric wires would set the leg off. Certain foods would zap me. I couldn't keep a laptop or hold a computer in my hands or lap without getting lit up. The more I did physically, the more the leg zapped me. Now, I'm going to tell you something that's just wrong, damn it. Every time I urinate my leg jumps up with bolts, every time. What's even worse, and this may be more info than you want, but I spit the whole truth out so you're getting it. Every time I have an orgasm it's followed by intense pain. As you can imagine I don't care much for sex anymore.

The two-year anniversary finally arrives and I'm still having these bolts all day long. *Just be patient*, I'm told. I say *Screw this* and we start looking around to see if there's another doctor or soul who can help me out with this problem. I see doctors in North Carolina, New York, Massachusetts, and Florida with absolutely no improvement. I'm telling you, it's like once they couldn't figure it out they just say, "Okay, nothing we can do." Then they give you the old *That can't be happening*. It's like they didn't believe me or thought that I was exaggerating. Then there were some who flat out didn't believe what I was saying. *Holy shit you dumb doctors, have you not been listening to anything I'm saying? Do you think I'm just making this stuff up for shits and giggles?*

On top of this I can't play much golf. Golf was the reason I'm fighting the fight. I'm trying to help others whose life gets thrown an asteroid. I'm doing it because I want to pull off a miracle on the course too. Dual goals of encouragement. I can't even do that. The more I do, the more pain I feel. I would survive through the day but once I got home and the leg came off I went into orbit. I said *Screw it, if I get into some events I'm going to play and suffer because I think it's too important to show others that you can overcome anything and get through it*. I mean, I was the best example on earth. I actually failed once when life threw me into a deep depression and I somehow survived. Now, with many more asteroids screaming right at me, this time I was going to show others struggling that it's okay to fail as long as we get our fat asses back up and continue the fight.

But the pain was costing me some events along with some speaking engagements and a few other ways I was going to try and inspire others. I'm on 150mg of Fentanyl along with my oxycontin pills, which only get me up and sometimes through the day. However, when the nerves go into overdrive I'm done. There wasn't anything out there that was going to stop these nerves from going nuts. Unless they knocked me out. But their lawyers weren't going to allow that. I probably was in the hospital every month or so and not once would they just knock me out. I would be yelling at them to just put me in a coma for a few hours damnit. *No, no sir, we can't do that, that's only for someone who's in horrific pain.* Sorry, you no good *&$#%@. I'm twitching and flipping like a hyena on meth and I'm not in enough pain for you pissheads? To this day doctors in hospitals disgust me.

It's Friday, December 22, 2017, and I'm getting ripped apart. I go to the hospital where I was just a few months back, hoping they would just grab my records from the last visit and things would go smoother. I'm a dumbass idiot at times. Common sense doesn't live at Palms West Hospital in Royal Palm Beach Florida. I'm getting prepped by the nurse and I'm twitching like a mad cow with a lob-wedge up his ass. She sees I'm in pain. The doctor comes out and starts to ask why I'm there. I ask him to look at my last visits and we can cut a lot of Baloney Time.

"No, why are you here?"

"I'm in nasty pain and it's going to get worse," I explain.

"So you have chronic pain then? We won't give you any narcotics at all," he says.

"What are you talking about?!"

"Opioid addictions are killing people and we can't do it."

I want to stick my foot in his ass but I'm trying to reason with him like a normal Ken Green would.

He says, "You need to leave."

"Wait, are you calling me a drug addict? You're a hospital, you're supposed to help me. Just go look at my damn file please."

"No, you need to leave."

I got up and said, "I'm going home now to self-medicate because the addicted druggie in front of you has amassed many, many patches of Fentanyl because he hates being on this stuff and the times he's been feeling well enough he doesn't use his patches, again because he hates being on this stuff, but he's collected over three months' worth of extras, waiting for the day some stupid-ass doctor refuses to help him. But your powers of perception must indeed be spot-on because it's very common for opioid addicts to go to the hospital for medical advice when they have three months' worth of opioids sitting in their closet. Asshole."

Then I told him that I have no idea how my body will handle all I'm going to give it, mixed with the pills, but if my body shuts down and I die, you son of a bitch, you won't give a fuck, will you?

I went home and suffered some of the worst bolts I can remember in the past eight years. I put on seven extra patches for a total of 800mg of fentanyl, plus twenty extra oxy pills and still suffered for 12 more hours. I get we have a drug issue in this country, but where is the common sense, damn it? I just can't explain it well enough and I'm not sure if you could even come close to understanding unless you went through some of it. I'm not sure why I'm putting this in the book, but truth be told I guess I want you to try and understand how much pain I was really in. I just kept yelling and screaming while curled up like a flaming gummy bear. Listen to people complain when they're in pain. What I've endured is just insane and was very likely preventable because of my idiot doctor in Mississippi, at Jackson Memorial Hospital.

The two great ladies I've been with during this period of pain are really the only ones who really know what intense pain I was going through. They got to see the twitching, seizure-like bouncing, stump-on-fire, and tears. They also got to see my refusal to quit no matter what I went through. They got to witness the stubborn-ass I really am and how it has benefited me this time around. Again, not sure why I'm telling you this, but maybe I want you, if you ever see me, to just come up and give me hug and say god bless you or something.

To give you a third-party point of view, I asked my ex-girl-friend Kristin to put something down about her experience with Mr. Pain. This is what she said:

"First off I want to let you all know how honored I am that Ken has allowed me to say a few words regarding the man I know and love. I was first drawn to Ken due to his unique ability to just be himself. He stunned me when he showed up on our first date with his dog Munch, wearing a pair of shorts and a T-shirt with animals on it. *What kind of first date am I getting into?* I asked myself.

Five hours later I knew he was special. Ken is afflicted with that rarest of personality traits: being open and honest. He has an uncanny ability to literally let out his feelings and then release them from his mind so as not to interfere with his inner self. I remember him warning me about his pain the very first time we met but if I must tell you the truth I really wasn't concerned because I was a hospice social worker and see pain everyday. I was soon to realize that his pain was not your ordinary pain. I will honestly say I've never seen a person endure this intense pain for so long yet he kept up the greatest front imaginable. His spirit has only waned a few times which is remarkable. I would watch him, knowing the leg was burning him, smile and laugh with hospital patients, and even give speeches to people without letting them know he was suffering. I've seen him get thrown from spot A to spot B six feet away like a bolt of lightning struck him in a split second. Literally thrown off his feet. It's truly difficult to explain his pain but it was excruciating for him. I was with him when doctors would come up with no conclusions or worse, not even believe him that the pain was so severe. I'm not sure any soul has had to endure as much as he has in one life, or lost so much, but I know in my heart God knew he could."

Now it's been a few weeks and I'm told I should be able to go home in few days. Shelley decides to leave knowing I'm getting out soon because her daughter Ashley is about to have a child. Just before I'm supposed to leave they come to me and tell me I've developed an infection in the stump area and they have to cut me open and clean me out. "Sure, knock yourself out," I said, figuring it par for the course at this point.

I woke up and damn it hurts like a mother's goat. So I'm stuck in the hospital for a few more days. Not like I'm going to go run the marathon, I rationalize, so it's fine. Times about up and low and behold they come to tell me the infection is back. Now I'm getting a little pissed.

Since Shelley left, my good friend Jerry 'Dub' Wygant was staying there to keep me company. They cut me open again and we go through the waiting period again. A few more days go by as I'm recovering from my second infection in five days. Then they come in and tell me there's still more infection and they have to open me up again! Are you kidding me? Wtf is going on here? "Three's a charm I hear, so fine, get it over with," I tell them.

The third time was a charm all right. Not only did the infection come back again, I ended up with TWELVE total surgeries to solve the infection issue. I ended up in the hospital for nine weeks of cut, slice, cut, cut, cut, slice. Not only did this hospital, Jackson Memorial in Jackson, Mississippi, screw everything up while I was there but they massively fucked up my life and career for the next eight years with their negligence. I shall explain...

The pain I went through over those nine years is something no one should ever have to go through, especially in a non-third-world country. For those of you fifty or older I will describe one of my two pains like this. Do you recall the feeling when you might have put your finger in a socket when you were a kid? Well, my leg did that every second for seven plus years with different levels of severity. I learned to deal with it because I was told I had no choice. At times, when it got to a level that even I couldn't handle, it would send me straight down to the ground. There were days I didn't move an inch. The first three years I had no surgeries because I was told the pain was normal. No one was listening to me about the zaps and the pain. I'm like *Fine, I guess, just don't be a cry-baby*, and I waited it out. Then for the next four years I had all sorts of surgeries and procedures—I had so many I still can't count them all. I had a spinal stimulator put in my back, they cut, burned and froze the nerves and none of it stopped the constant zapping.

I saw doctors from New York, North Carolina, D.C., Connecticut and Florida, and no one had any real answers as to why I'm still in such incredible pain, NINE YEARS AFTER MY ACCIDENT.

Then I get a call from Hawaii from my brother-in-law telling me about a procedure called the Ertl. This is a procedure where they build a "bone-bridge" to keep the two free hanging bones from moving all over and pressing against the nerves. "I'm in!" I say. I'll do anything at this point. I'm literally on the verge of calling it quits, the pain is just too much.

At this stage I'm on 150 mg of fentanyl (ten times stronger than morphine) and as much OxyContin as I need. So off to Kalamazoo, Michigan I fly to have Dr. Ertl's promising surgery. It is what I learn this week that will make me want to fly down to Mississippi and unleash some reckoning on those doctors and that hospital.

They roll me back to my room after surgery. I wake up and there is my love Kristin holding my hands. "How do you feel?" she asks.

"There's no zapping, none," I say. We both start crying. Seven-plus years and the zapping is finally gone.

"So the surgery was a success!" I yelled, tears streaming down my face.

Kristin looks at me and tells me that no, they actually never did do the surgery. I was confused. "What do you mean they didn't do the surgery, I feel fantastic!" I stuttered.

"They didn't need to do the surgery. They didn't have to take a bone from your good leg and use it to bridge your broken ones in your bad leg because your bad leg bone had already fused with another bone in your leg. It had done it all on its own," she relayed.

"Ahha!" I said. "You always said I didn't have a smart bone in my body, and here you are proven wrong," I gloated. But that still didn't explain why my zapping was gone.

The medical team then went on to explain:

•The bump in my eye was caused by a big piece of glass that was still stuck in there and was never removed after the accident.

•They found 10 neuromas (damaged and overgrown nerves) which were the reason for the zapping. TEN OF THEM. The nerves were four times the length they were supposed to be. They should have been handled at the time of surgery but they weren't and in 8 years they had grown to several inches instead of millimeters!

•They found a clamp that was left in after surgery that was still clamped to one of my nerves, which caused it to 'go off' every second, FOR SEVEN YEARS.

•They found a nerve stitched to a blood vessel. This is standard operating procedure for surgeries like mine but you HAVE to cut it off before you close the wound. A nerve stitched to a blood vessel is a prescription for constant and extreme pain.

"Is that it?" I cried.

"Isn't that enough?" she said.

I could not believe what I had just been told. I thought back to the time I had told the doctor to cut off my leg. I had known amputees and especially amputee golfers. I didn't know any of them that complained constantly about the pain. I thought I was a wimp and that I needed to just suck it up. And this whole time I had a nerve stitched to a blood vessel, a clamp clamped to one of my nerves inside my leg, a large piece of glass in my eye, and 10, TEN, neuromas of unbelievable length and potency sending painful shockwaves to my brain every second of every day for eight years. For fuck sakes how is this possible?!

Let's just say that what is quite possible is that in about two years I might be the proud owner of Jackson Memorial Hospital, if not half the State of Mississippi. Stay tuned on that front.

All the good I was hoping to do in terms of advocating for amputees and trying to compete in my Champions Tour comeback was delayed *eight years* due to total and complete incompetence. You can only imagine how I feel about that. If you don't, it's nothing less than devastating.

For the first time in almost eight years I am zap free. The other pains are still with me, and it's intense at times, but it comes and goes, so I think I can deal with it, but I definitely hate it with a passion.

When I left Dr. Ertl I was told that in one-percent of cases there can be over-active nerves and they could grow back to cause me some electrical zapping. Since I had 10 neuromas that percent increases to about 10%. I've started to have a few zaps here and there, but nothing like I was having before. It's more than a shame I left 8 years of a more regular life on that operating table in Mississippi.

Frankly, it's criminal.

23/

Last Chat with the King

Myself and the rest of the Green team (this week it was my Kristin and the five members of the Tourneime family from the deepest northern edge of upper Michigan) were in Madison for the Steve Stricker Champions Tour event. I was pretty wiped out from a long pro-am on a rather tough, hilly track, our whiffle ball game and our usual talk about everything and nothing.

That night I was sleeping like the proverbial gator. I woke up in the morning and immediately told Kristin and Joel's family the following: "I just had a conversation with the King." I then told them that the great Arnold Palmer would be dead in two months. I then proceeded to tell them exactly why and what happened. In my dream I'm in a room where I turn to see the King rocking in a wooden chair. He has an old-style yellow cardigan sweater on. "Arnie, what are you doing here?" I ask. "I'm here to tell you I'm going to be dead in two months," he says. "Why are you telling me this Arn?" "I'm telling you this because I can get through to you and tell you."

He kept rocking slowly as he told me this, all the while giving me the smile that he made famous. To this day I can see him clear as a bell in the chair and yellow sweater talking to me like it was today and not a couple of years ago. Some of you may believe this or you might think once again Ken has lost his marbles. I promise you on Munch's life it was real and I knew the King was going to be dead soon. This is how Joel Tourneime describes what happened next:

"It was later in the evening on September 25, 2016 when I heard on the Golf Channel that Arnold Palmer, The King, had passed away. My first reaction was, sadly, "Man, Ken's dreams came true."

Jumping back a few months, it was in June that the Champions Tour was in Madison, Wisconsin for Steve Stricker's inaugural hosting of The American Family Insurance tournament. Ken got into the field and had invited my family to spend the week with he and Kristin. We were hanging out at the house Ken had rented for the week one evening after the pro-am. Anyone who has been around a golf tournament knows that there are decent amounts of time to pass in the evenings, and Ken has led the way on more Nip Opens, dart games, whiffle ball battles, and car races than I can recall. So I was certainly surprised when he looked at me and said, "I'm worried that Arnold is going to pass away soon." What struck me was how serious and somber he was about it. Ken went on to tell me about the recent dream he had about Mr. Palmer. 'Even when he passes, he will forever be what gave golf life. Who's gonna possibly be able to take over for him?' Ken said. As serious as I have ever seen him, we just sat there in silence for a few moments. I guess some questions answer themselves.

The night Mr. Palmer died, Ken told me about how he kept having the dream since we had last seen him in June. He then went on to tell me again how fond he was of Mr. Palmer and how he had this way of just making everyone around him feel good about themselves. I remember thinking, 'Maybe I've finally heard a story about someone who loves golf more than Ken Green.'"

24/

Golf's Future and Technology

The media loves talking about how there are so many better athletes in today's game than in the past. Let me make
this perfectly clear: Yesterday's golfers were far more coor-
dinated than those of today. In general, all eras have some
super-studs, but you had to be really good to play pro golf with persimmon woods. Today the game is much easier; there are fewer ex-
ceptional all-round athletes playing golf as a result. And because the
game comes easier to them, at an earlier age, those same players don't
achieve much because they haven't learned how to score and win. Vi-
jay Singh had a great career. He is a product of technology. He sucked
in his twenties because he couldn't keep it on planet earth, much less
a golf course. He always had the brain to win but didn't have the skills
to get there until the clubs and ball became so good. He won most of
his events when guys like Jack were aging out of the game because
of the old equipment. Only technology lets you get better as you age.

Think about some good golfing friends you know today. Many
are better now than they were twenty years ago. It's not because they
have more time to work on their game- it's wholly because of technology. And the tech explosion has only helped the better golfers- the
under-8 handicap types. The poor 18-plus handicappers just keep getting worse as they age. In my view the thing that helped the great Phil
Mickelson finally win majors was technology. That man was really
good when he got out on the PGA Tour and won as an amateur. So

why didn't he win a major until he was 33? It had nothing to do with the "learning curve"- it was the equipment and the ball. He was, and still is, an aggressive player, and, like me, you paid dearly for aggressive shots gone bad in majors. I sucked in majors because I was more aggressive than Phil and too stupid to realize you can't compete in majors thinking you're Zorro.

I used to shake my head at the whining Sergio, the ultimate cry-baby. However, he eventually learned, and I respect that immensely. He stopped blaming others and became likeable again. He's the opposite of Phil- I think technology hurts his game. He's one of the better ball-strikers so he would benefit from other players' missed shots in majors if the damn ball didn't straighten itself out so much. The driver and the putter may be the trickiest shots under big pressure. I suggest that his driver would be basically the same but the inferior ball strikers now get away with mediocre swings that today are still in the fairway where in earlier years you would miss the fairway completely, which in majors usually means bogey or worse.

Jack won a couple of majors in his forties, but I promise you if he had had today's equipment in his forties he would have won five or six. They say that he's one of the best putters ever and he lagged putts into the hole. Give him today's greens and he would've putted as good or better than Tiger did. Go putt on a quick, bumpy, spike-marked green and tell me how the hell he made any putts, much less win 18 majors. It's my belief that Jack wins 28 majors and finishes second nine times instead of the 19 he did, if he had today's greens in his prime. He's still considered the best long-iron player of all time. So how good would he hit today's hybrids? Sam Snead, who was a complete jerk, would've been a super-stud with today's stuff.

If today's golfers are so much better, and better athletes, why isn't one of those players of the last twenty years not considered in the top ten of ball strikers? Go look at the "fluke" winners of the past twenty years versus say the seventies or sixties. I promise you that Michael Campbell never wins the U.S. Open with equipment of the 90s or earlier. Pre-1990s, Orville "fluke" Moody won his only PGA Tour event in 1969, which was the U.S. Open, because he was a great ball striker. He should've putted with a square ball and maybe he would've made more putts.

Putting is so easy today it's scary. So why are there not lower winning scores when the greens are softer, courses play shorter, and the rough is cut so short? Do they lose motivation with having ten million in the bank after two good years? Today's stud players have the distance control of a mosquito. Miller, Hogan, Snead, Jack and many others were insane when they were on. Miller was the best- he would be inside 15 feet on 14 holes. You never see that today. Why?

Two things come to mind: Is the hard ball too hard to control, or is the speed they swing today to blame? I sucked at ball striking but from the fairway with a seven-iron I knew as soon as I hit it how far it was going to fly, and I would typically be only a yard or so off of that distance. I'm stunned a teacher doesn't have one of his players slow down the intensity of his or her iron swings to learn distance control. Dustin Johnson got so much better once he decided to fix his wedges. He is today's Johnny Miller in some ways. (On the course only though). When DJ gets it going he is tough to beat, yet he, like Miller, can't get the ball in the hole on the greens. He could be unbelievable if he knew how to putt. He should putt like he bangs other people's wives: Don't think, just get it in the hole.

REASONS FOR GOLF'S DOOM

TECHNOLOGY
I'm not simply talking about golf technology here, but technology in general. The computer age has created way too many spoiled-ass parents who are more concerned about themselves than their kids. They let the screen mesmerize the kids- babysit them basically, because they don't want to be parents. Not everyone is this way, so please calm your itchy Twitter fingers, but many. So now we have kids who will spend hours beating up video games and will finish one in a week or two. Golf will own you until you die, and then it will own everyone you've ever known until they die. You may come out on top a week here and a week there, but golf will just drive you nuts the rest of your days and that's why you fall in love with golf. But today's kids don't have the patience or temperament to fall in love with golf. It's a really hard game and they don't have the temperament to stay with it and try and take it on. They run to the computers where we can hack off the heads of zombies or Tim Finchump (has that game been developed yet because I can think of one person who would buy it).

The second aspect of tech is the equipment. *How in the world does better equipment help bring on the demise of golf,* you ask? It brought us harder courses, which makes it really hard for the average Joe newcomers, so they just quit playing. The courses are expected to be in better shape, and most are, but at a much higher cost, which the average player pays for. The greens should be the main concern on a golf course. Tees will be mats one day so why not now? Bunkers need to become almost extinct. Good golfers love bunkers—they're easy as hell for us. They're nightmares for most golfers, and then they add time to the round with raking, and the inevitable leaving of one or two shots in the bunker. Bunkers were originally supposed to be a shot or half-shot added to your score, but today they're so well maintained and manicured it's like stealing for pros. Make most of them grass bunkers, which the pros don't like but the average guy won't even blink at when in there. And this doesn't even go into the fact that bunkers are one of the most expensive labor sinkholes on a golf course. Make them grass bunkers and save tens of thousands of bucks a year for already cash-strapped courses. Unfortunately, a move like this takes nuggets and most course managers and owners lack even one.

GREED

The greatest curses of life, in my view, are money, greed, power and ego. The expense of the game of golf has hurt so many people it's crazy. This will come off as politically incorrect at best so be warned: The lower middle income and poor souls who might have caddied or played the ugly nine-hole tracks don't anymore because there are not as many caddies or crappy courses. I grew up on the worst nine-hole track on earth, but when you're young and learning, that doesn't bother you. Unfortunately, in today's social media atmosphere where everyone is a know-it-all and critic, most people won't bother with those crappy courses so they just skip golf, period. The young kids who are patient enough now can't get to even play those little, cheap nine-hole tracks because they are nowhere to be found. Can you think of a better way to keep a young kid busy after school than playing golf? It's perfect. Unfortunately, the cost of playing golf is ridiculous today, and it's time to blame some who don't ever share in any of the blame: PGA Tour players.

Today's tour players are paid so much by golf companies it's insane. The average Sam or Sally eventually pays for the cost of these contracts, just like insurance companies pass their losses onto the policy holders. Three hundred dollars for a forking putter?! You can buy a lot of groceries for $300. The putter will bring you only misery, while the groceries, well, you get the point. If Karsten Solheim of PING were alive today he would never abandon the average golfer, he would help keep prices down.

Advertising is another cost that's gone haywire and again the average Tom and Tammy pays for it. The golf companies come out with new drivers and stuff every year now, and each time it's "the best ever." The golfer is always looking for that miracle driver that gives them an extra 10-15 yards. The odds of finding that driver are like winning the lotto but golfers are always searching for that special weapon that will help their game. So we fall prey and keep buying the new stuff, only to be disappointed again and again. *And that's the people who can afford the new stuff.* There's a huge number of golfers who love the game but can't keep pouring money into their game, so that not only keeps them away but discourages them from even playing if they're certain their equipment sucks. And they *know* their equipment sucks because the manufacturers have been telling them their equipment sucks since they literally walked out of the store with their new purchase. It's a cycle that's killing this game.

The pace that PGA Tour players play has also affected the length of the game, which many feel has hurt golf. Understand this: Tour players don't care if they are slow or hurting the game, they will take all the damn time they want to 'read' putts, regardless of whether it's actually helpful or not. It's a proven fact that the best putters in the world don't line up their putts correctly. Say a player has a 15-footer and wants to play a cup outside right edge. He will miss that spot 90 percent of the time, not by much, but they miss it almost all the time! So now, instead of aiming a cup right, he's a cup and an inch right. Then he's got to hit the right speed that he read for the line, which as we now know, is the wrong line 90 percent of the time. And pros are off half the time with their speed, which is good, but still a glaring issue, especially when the intended speed is wrong for the intended line 90 percent of the time. Now, add to that the fact that we pull and push some putts as well. We're the best in the world and we make these errors often, so why on earth do we have to take that much time reading a damn putt?!

In February of 2019 at the Genesis Open in Los Angeles, J.B. Holmes took over two minutes to hit a 40-footer, which he managed to send 15 feet beyond the hole. I guess he should have taken four minutes to get it 7.5 feet past.

How many of you get over a putt and just know it's going in? Then you make it and realize you barely even read the putt. So, imagine your slow-ass donkey-head amateur golfer who makes five times the errors pros make. The average golfer might hit his line once out of eighty putts—or once every two rounds! Add to that the fact that an average golfer's speed is never right, and we won't even get into the pure strokes he or she never makes. So why the hell do you take so long to putt, damn it? Take a quick look at the line and trust your feel. I promise, the less you try the better you will play. The harder we try, the more we fuck up. How many of you have played great rounds with that little buzz from alcohol? It blocks the demons. That's why they've banned the beta blocker pills from golf. Just ask John Daly.

USGA, PGA, ROYAL & ANCIENT

The powers who should be sounding the alarm about golf's decline are saying just the opposite, it seems. They are preaching how great golf is today. That's the Bob Rotella (and other sports docs) theory, who preached the Never Think or Say Bad Thoughts or You Will Fail. *Holy shit?!* If you fart in a closed car your friends say *Wtf dude!* They don't say *Hey farter, it's cool this fart was so close to being a non-smelling fart, and we're so close to our destination, that you're right on the edge of attaining pure fartvanah, and non-stained underwear to boot. We are all just going to enjoy the aroma, take it all in!*

Truth is the best way out of a hole. The deniers are nothing but one massive fat-ass-ostrich-with-head-firmly-planted-in-sand. Trickle-down economics is in full force. The PGA Tour believes everything is hunky dory because the purses are huge (thanks Tiger) and their players are swimming in sponsor and manufacturer dollars, and that those two barometers are accurate indicators of the health of the game. But in twenty years, when the Millennials are the CEO's running corporate America, and they've never touched a golf club in their lives, does the tour really think purses will be what they are today and the game will be as 'healthy' as they claim it is? Yes, they will, because see: Bob Rotella Theory. This is idiocy.

The pro tours and golf will take a beat-down at that point. None of the game's supposed caretakers have come up with new ideas on how we can bring and keep new golfers to the game. They have hundreds of millions of dollars, yet they do nothing to help golf grow. Why? The USGA just made changes to some rules and had commercials saying how it was going to help the game and its pace. Five minutes to find a ball is now going down to three minutes. Wow, saving 2 minutes a round! "Wheeee, did you hear that ma?! I'm going to take up golf now," said no one ever. And what golfer do you know will say, "Hey, times up, you have to stop looking." The dropping procedure has been moved from shoulder height to knee height. What golfer drops the ball the right way now anyway, you idiots? Now you can tamp down spike marks and practically anything else on the greens. That will certainly add time to the round, not shorten it! I think their heads should be tamped down.

There have to be changes that will allow the golfer to hit better shots as beginners and make it more fun so you get psyched about your next round. Unless you reach the level of, say, a 23-handicap you should tee up every ball, everywhere. It's really hard for the average newcomer to hit the ball off the ground, especially on courses that cost less than $50 to play. It's discouraging for young kids and they quit. I really think kids should be allowed to play two-ball scramble every time until they reach a certain level. They will feel better about the good shots and get psyched to get better. Plus, they get more swings, and who doesn't like that when you're young? It will have no effect on pace of play either.

I would love to use a six-inch hexagon-shaped cup instead of the round four-inch cup. The purists can be appeased by allowing the old cup for pro events. We have to make the game a tad easier to keep today's maybe-golfers happy and psyched about coming back tomorrow. The mental edge will help so many because the shape of the hexagon cup will look so much bigger, and combined with the new flag-in rules, the hole will look like the Grand Canyon. The mental golfer is usually shitting his pants over the five-footers. Truth be told, I believe we should not use a hole at all. We need to use a bottle-like tube that will ting when it's hit by a ball. Go putt to a bottle the same size of the hole and watch how much better you will putt thinking you only have to nick it. I know that's a dream but it would work to help hackers stay in the game.

Tour players are actually part of the reason golf is sliding. *Wtf did you just say Green?* Well, look at it like this. Jordan Spieth gets one million for showing up at the Australia Open and he pockets it. Well, if the players and agents weren't so damn greedy and thought they needed $200 million to live on, versus say $50 million, why don't they take some of that money and help golf courses and new players. Many have charitable foundations and that's great, but where is the urge to help golf? We need golfers. Let's say Spieth gives one or two million a year to a course he buys, or a city owns. He then takes care of all expenses with that money. Now, they set up a program where every parent pays zero if they show up with their kids. Then you implement the new Ken Green rules (new cup, mat tees, grass bunkers, etc.) and you accomplish family unity along with growing golf. Then you multiply that with all the other pros and sponsors all over America and you now have hundreds of thousands of new rounds for new or existing golfers. Many will fall in love with golf and move on and some won't, but who cares, we'll have new people in the game. A subsidized course in Dallas would probably pull in fifty thousand rounds, and that's a lot of new people playing golf. This can easily be done in so many cities it's scary.

Warren Buffet could set up one hundred courses for life if he put in $2 billion of his dollars he swears he's going to give away (supposedly giving away something like $30 billion) when the old fork goes belly up. I mean he's 85 or so, so why not do it now? It's not like he can't live on $30 billion, right? Is there a faster or better way to get thousands of families together and help golf? None that I know of, especially something that families can do for the rest of their years.

They all talk about helping diseases, which again is great, but everyone says our family unity is dying and it's a main reason why so many kids are screwed up, so why not start programs where we save the healthy but broke families and give them family structure and family time together? Maybe we become the very first athletes that actually have a real and immediate impact on families and their lives. Do the math on how many kids and families would be impacted by these policies. Then for those who want their name to live in infamy, their names would stay on those courses and educational clubhouses forever. Because like it or not Jack Nicklaus is the only name anyone will still remember in 100 years, with an occasional *Hey who was that black golfer who was lights out until he had a train wreck with his*

9-iron? Then again, maybe I'm short-selling myself and they will also know the infamous one-legged stud-idiot golfer that helped save the game of golf. I'm as dumb as you can get, but damn this is a no forking brainer: A way to reach thousands of people and keep them together. The cheap-ass Tiger Woods could do wonderful projects with his cash and could really make incredible headway in a world where father figures are disappearing and incarceration rates are skyrocketing. We can develop programs where those kids get help at the learning centers that are at these courses, and they will be exposed to all kinds of father figures there to boot. Damn it, get off your asses tour players and help save the game that has made you so wealthy. I promise you that when the rich are on their death-bed they don't say to their kids "Gee, I'm sorry I screwed up, I should have worked more and made more money, and I spent way too much time with you guys and I'm sorry about that." They say the exact opposite. So here's a moron telling you now to stop, and think, and help others get on the golf course.

SELFISH PARENTS AND COACHES
The wisdom of today says you must focus on only one sport. Parents and coaches make these poor kids practice and play that one sport four, five, six times a week like they're pros making a living. The four-sport athletes are gone, two sports are rare. Is it the parents or coaches? I'm not sure, but damn, what happened to just having fun playing sports? If your child is going to the big time they will get there damn it. There are more injuries now than ever. Is it the crazy-ass coach who thinks he's Joe Stud and will get new jobs at the next level, or is it the parent dreaming of money or college scholarships coming to save them from their own irresponsibility of not saving for college? I know you people don't see that in yourselves, but damn it, let your kids have fun.

Many golf clubs today are run by 40- and 50-year-olds who are so selfish they don't want to give any time to kids or kids' golf events. What in the hell is the matter with you people? Golf is the greatest game on earth and does more for business and charity than all others combined. So get off your selfish greedy asses and start doing something for golf and others, damn it. Every private club sells their course on Monday to charity events to raise cash so their spoiled selfish souls don't have to cough up any more money in dues. Damn it, give your course up for nothing once a month and be nice about it. Better yet, do it for every charity outing. I once suggested when I was in the media tent at Augusta National playing The Masters that they should hold a raffle every year for the average guy. Who wouldn't pay 10 or 20 bucks to have a chance to win one of 75 spots to play at Augusta? It would be a memory of a lifetime. Think about if a person who loves golf and watches The Masters every year won a spot to play- it would without a doubt be their greatest day alive.

One of the best things the PGA Tour does is raise money for charity. So why are private clubs not doing the same thing? Greed and selfishness. The great Winged Foot charges $1,000 per person to hold a charity gig there, and they're fully booked. I'm pretty sure most of the members are doing pretty well so why not say *Hey, we're going to open our course to kids more and to charities that are involved with golf and kids only. We want to give Average Joe Public a chance at playing our great course.* Every golfer owes it to golf and its future to stop being so selfish and greedy. We need to grow golf, not kill it. I have personal friends whom I love dearly but don't get it. We have to help golf and we can do it by helping kids. It's like a quadruple win-win-win-win. I love Ridgewood Country Club in Danbury, and many of my friends I love are members. Yet I can't convince any of them that growing the sport is more important than money. Just Ken Green screaming into the abyss once more.

GOLF COMPANIES

The companies who will tell you they care and want golf to grow are a part of the reason it's dying. They do want it to grow absolutely, but they are a part of its demise. Their costs have gone up for sure, but they are paying pros way too much money. I'm sorry, you will never convince me that Rory will sell $10 million a year worth of clubs, or Spieth, Phil, or any of the stars. Not even Tiger Mania paid off. Tiger didn't bring golfers to the game like many thought he would. He brought viewers to the game. We had more minorities on tour in the 70s and 80s than they have there now! That math is simple, even for me. And even the superstar brands of Nike and Tiger Woods couldn't succeed, as Nike left the golf business with Tiger as their No. 1 endorser.

Then you add the fact that they bring out new clubs at least once a year and selling golfers on the fallacy that this year's driver is five times better than last year's, and you can see how this will kill the desire of the casual golfer. And then the marketing costs are more than any other era so their costs are much higher, which means the average guy has to pay for these babies. Five hundred for a driver or three hundo for a putter is just wrong. The cold, hard fact is that only the 8-handicap or better really gets any benefit from today's technology. If you sucked ten years ago you probably still suck. I have friends who are good golfers but are just that, good. They're better now, twenty-plus years later. It's not because they're working on their game more, it's purely technology. I have other friends who sucked back in the eighties and suck even more now because they just don't have the golf skills or the cash to take advantage of the tech boom. So as they aged, they got worse. The decent guy can get better or hold off Father Time as he ages because of technology.

The last phony-sell by companies and us tour players is the putter- that if you don't have the perfect balance or weight or toe angle you're doomed. Folks, confidence is the only thing you really ever need when putting. No one starts the ball where they want to anyway, much less reads it right or judges the speed correctly so why the hell do we need that perfect putter for three hundred dollars or more? Corey Pavin is still a great putter with the old Bulls Eye putter from the seventies. It's the ugliest thing on earth and looks like an anorexic stick but he makes everything because he believes he's going to. In the late 90s Phil was putting with something that looked like a pole axe left over from the Crimean War. Confidence, speed, and trust is all you need to be a good putter.

WHAT WOULD DICTATOR GREEN DO TO SAVE GOLF?

I have some standard ideas and some that only the Green mind might come up with, so first let me tell you how we save golf and bring the younger people into the game. The obvious ideas are just that, and they're not working, so I'm going to stick with the Green Ideas.

There are hundreds of millions of dollars donated to The First Tee programs. It's a wonderful concept of teaching kids ethics and an improved moral compass, which is great, but in my opinion they have not even come close to producing the number of golfers for the money they are pulling in each year. Those in charge of The First Tee have spent way too much money for what they've accomplished and in any normal business if the results aren't there, neither are you for long. Except of course if it's an organization with Tim Finchem at the helm, then everyone gets to fail upward.

My thoughts on The First Tee are this: You can keep the program but you must add these few pieces, which would be huge, in my view. First, you have to have a much bigger building where there will be classes and computers for the kids. They will be taught what they're not taught in school; common freaking sense along with real-life issues that will come up, including how you handle money and how to survive once you're on your own. It would include the class, "How To Speak to Humans," and kids would learn how to keep one's composure when things don't go your way, which might be the biggest lesson in life. And perhaps some school work. You develop a bussing system that kids can take from schools on their allotted days to come to the facility. They will be given credits for attending and improving their skills through golf as well as the other things taught at The First Tee. After all, isn't The First Tee an analogy for life? *It's the First freaking Tee for a reason!*

Kids will also be taught about golf agronomy and nature and why golf course are better for the environment than most people believe. Then they will golf and have fun. I would create new, fun holes like I do for my Nip Opens. What kid wouldn't like hitting or playing a hole where you must first ricochet it off a wall or through a window or skip it on the water, or where you hit it over the house or under the cow. Mini golf gone steroidal, I guess. They will love it and then those who fall for the game will golf for life and those who don't move on, and that's okay because when they get older they'll find out golf is a good way to have fun or enjoy family or customers, etc. But at least they'll have held a golf club in their hands and will have learned at least something from their time at The First Tee.

I would find nine- or 18-hole courses and lower the fees as low as they can go. We make this possible by implementing mat tees, four sand bunkers (the rest grass bunkers) and a bunch of crazy fun holes scattered about, all managed by a staff of only three or four people. We devise a program where the kids take care of the course, which will obviously teach them so many things for the future it's incredible. We support this 3-4 employee golf course by implementing a program for local companies or the city, or The First Tee, to support the course. Each hole can be sponsored by a local company. I would have a program where kids play for free and if a parent comes with them, they pay five bucks. The school teachers and others who help with the kids also get to play for free. I'm a firm believer that if we do things together as a group, people we will stay together and keep it together. What better way to get multiple racial and socio-economic groups together and working for the betterment of their community?

I would hope to find a golf company that will make a "super ball." I want beginners and many ladies and older men to be able to play a ball that goes 20 yards farther. They must feel good about what they're doing. What fun can a 67-year-old woman have driving the ball 110 yards? Let's make that puppy fly 150 yards damn it! It's not like the USGA is going to have a Menopausal Invitational any time soon. We need to have fun. Golf is hard you know.

I would use the hexagon cup and the bottle cup on every green. I would love to have a six-inch bottle cup. All you have to do is hit it. No lip outs, no panic, just hit it. When every player gets good enough they can go to the next level.

I need one of you billionaires who love golf, family, kids, and the United States of America, to cough up $100 million and I promise you I will start the revolution that saves golf, family, kids and the good ole' USA!

10 QUICK GREEN RULES FOR SAVING GOLF

1- Until you break 100, you tee up every ball, everywhere
2- Eliminate par. Just keep your score on each hole. Max on any hole is 8, your final score is the only thing that matters
3- Each golfer gets two mulligans per nine
4- Talk, sing, heckle whenever you want
5- Must have a competitive game every time
6- You learn to win or lose each day; dollars, underwear, sexy pics, lawn mowing hours, anything else you can come up with
7- One shot penalty for every water or OB and drop the ball where it went in
8- Newcomers play bottle cup or hex-hole until they break 100, whichever is closer after the ball is hit onto the green
9- My ideal course would have six par threes, all different distances
10- At least two CRAZY GREEN holes per nine

25/

Quickies

The PGA of America gave Tom Watson and I the Comeback Player of the Year in 2010. The question I have is: Why did they lie? They said it was a tie. So either they wanted Tom there to give a speech at The Masters (where the title is awarded) or they forgot about me and someone said, "Hey, shoulder surgery versus what happened to Ken Green is not really comparable." Why does the most honest game going have people at the top who just lie? Even Tom said it in his speech: "I'm not really sure why I'm here." The PGA of America is run by fellow pros who get elected to the job. Sadly, I've never met a pro who is happy with the work the PGA of America does. They are a very greedy organization and have made choices for money over what's right for their pros and fans.

We should ban all men from the U.S. political system. Men have screwed it up. It's time to see if women can work together and do a better job.

If Buffet, Gates and other billionaires want to give half their money away why not do it now? One is 80-plus and the other 60-plus. Can they not make it on $30 billion?

⛳The last year I went to Sun City in South Africa it was kind of a fun fest. I was pissed because my soon-to-be-ex-wife Ellen broke her word to me that the whole family was going and we were going to do the tourist thing. One night after the dreaded black-tie gala I ended up gambling and having fun with a lady who was not Ellen. She was drop-dead gorgeous. We ended up in her room at about five in the morning and before we could start having fun, I decided I just couldn't do it. We chatted until 6:30 a.m., one hour before my tee time. I jumped up, gave her a kiss goodbye and bolted out of the room to shower and get ready. I took about 20 steps and ran right into Bernhard Langer coming out of his room. "Hey Bern, how's it going?" I said, still dressed in my fine black-tie gear. "See you in a few," I said as he looked at me kind of baffled. I was playing with him that day. Little did he know I was trying to bring back the dress code from the 1920's. I beat him that day-he sucked at putting and those greens were as good as you could get back then. Ellen and I split right after I got back. Damn my semi-integrity.

⛳The PGA Championship at Shoal Creek was eventually won by Wayne "he lost to me at the Buick Open" Grady. Ellen was flying in the night before and had a flight from hell. The small-plane flight from Atlanta to Birmingham was petrifying. She wasn't real happy but was glad to be alive. We teed off at about 9 a.m. so I got there with my usual thirty minutes to spare. I walked into the locker room and put my flashy green shoes on and off I went to the range. I got there and brother Bill looked at me weirdly.

"What's up?" I said.

"Well, for starters, we teed off 30 minutes ago," he revealed.

Shit, how?

Then a lightbulb went off. I only looked at my time from the *USA Today* paper which posted in Eastern time and I never saw the time anywhere else. Brother Bill, my caddie, never bothered to look either. The buck stops with me but I'll throw 60 percent of the blame to him. I walked over to Ellen and explained what had happened. She was not happy. Bill Glasson was though, since he got in.

The PGA won by Payne Stewart in 1989 was held at Kemper Lakes in Chicago. I had to take Brad and Brooke to Chicago by myself because Ellen refused to go because that's when she decided to get a boob job. Not one week later, but right in the middle of a major. So after suffering another loss in the argument department I said I would take the kids with me. We had a blast that week until Friday. This was an era when we didn't have full-blown childcare on tour like we do now. The PGA said they would keep the kids no later than 6 o'clock. They never planned on a rain delay. Well, the rain delay came and once I realized I wasn't going to be able to pick the kids up by 6pm I told my playing partner, Davis Love III, that I was withdrawing. He looked at me quizzically. I then told him my story and he just said, "Oh shit." His wife Robin also heard the story and immediately offered to pick up my kids. I was very thankful and finished the round wondering what a dope I am.

The Pensacola Open is the one that got away. I played really good golf that week. I was tied for the lead going into the last hole and the leader still had a few holes to play. The 18th green was a two-tier green, left side high, right side low, which is unusual for sure. The pin was about ten feet from the edge. The smart play was to hit my 6-iron, 180-yards out, to the left side of the green for a certain par. I'm just not too smart. Intelligence just isn't in my DNA. I decided to hit a shot right at it. I hadn't made a bogey all week, by the way. I hit a damn good shot. I missed my target by five feet. It flew five feet right of the intended target, which was five feet right of the pin. The green sloped left to right so when it hit dead-on-line about ten feet short it rolled to the right and hung on the edge. Then it rolled dead down the hill to about seventy feet. One three-putt later and I picked up my second-place prize. It was a good shot hit by a dumb player. The reason I never played well in majors is because I was too aggressive and you just can't do that in majors because you pay dearly. I told you intelligence isn't in my DNA. (Ironically, a very similar shot at the 1989 Ryder Cup would lead to a very similar result).

Another one that got away from me was the 1988 GGO in Greensboro, North Carolina. I had just made five birdies on the back nine to catch and pass Sandy Lyle, who had a good lead starting the day. The last birdie was on 17 so I was one up going into the last hole. I hit a perfect drive on the tough driving hole which was followed by a pulled eight-iron to 45 feet. I then hit my first putt four feet short. I wasn't concerned one bit as I just had six one-putts in the last eight holes. Just as I was starting my follow through a big gust of wind hit my pants and the right pant leg flapped and I flinched just a tad and missed the putt. (If I had been wearing the skin-tight pants of today I definitely would have made it). I had to make a five-footer coming back. Lyle then birdied the first playoff hole and that was that. I did win the next year though, to get some revenge. Just some.

I've been fortunate to do 2.5 golf course designs. Twenty-seven holes in Albuquerque, New Mexico, with Ken Killian. It turned out to be a very good course for the small budget we had. I vehemently argued with five designs of greens saying they were too sloped and would leave very few pin location options. The owner went with Killian who said they would be fine. I believe they played a Web Tour event there. Oh, and he had to rebuild those greens a couple years later. The other design I did was with John Sanford called The Quest in Houghton Lake, Michigan. Once again, a very small budget, but it to came out really nicely. I also did a redo of nine holes at Breakers West in West Palm Beach. I'm here to tell you that you can build a course that would be hard for good players but Joe Average would walk off saying *It's not that hard why didn't I shoot lower?* I have no clue why architects haven't figured this out yet. I'm no genius, damn it.

I've mentioned the two months of alimony ($27,000) debt to Ellen and my arrest warrant. What I didn't mention was how I became a money launderer. When I left the casino and drove back to my friend's house, Sir Wayne McElree in Danbury, Connecticut, I had lots of cash. Upon arriving late that night I knew I was golfing early that Sunday so I needed a place to stick my cash in case his house got robbed, though highly unlikely. I decided I would stick it into my pillow case of dirty laundry. I mean, who would steal smelly-ass clothes, right? I finished my round and walked into the house knowing I was going to see Hunter that week when I returned Monday and paid off my debt (hence all the cash in my possession). I walked into a smirking McElree. *What's up?* He then told me he decided to be a nice guy and threw my pillowcase straight into the washer and then the dryer. When he opened the dryer he had hundred dollar bills flying out of the machine. He was stunned and laughing. He then told me I had $25,800 in clean one-hundred-dollar bills upstairs along with my clean shirts. I'm like, "McElree, there was $27,000 and we need to find the rest or I'm screwed. I have to pay this alimony or I won't be able to see Hunter." We bolted to the dryer where I eventually found the 12 bills stuck into the machine in all the places hundred-dollar bills hide in a dryer.

After another successful visit to Foxwoods I had $60,000 in cash and again I was staying with a now married McElree and his wife Melissa. I was there for another week and then I went south. Two weeks later I got a call from my buddy asking if I had left anything at the house. I said knowing me, I'm sure I did. *What did I leave now?* I asked. He then proceeded to tell me that Melissa went up to clean the room after her parents had stayed over and she pulled out a bag from a drawer and low and behold there was sixty grand in the bag. "Oh shit yes," I said. I had forgotten about it and left it there. Scary how I just forgot about that kind of money, but I did.

26/

I Lost a Leg and the Tour
Lost Their Marbles

When I made the decision to cut the leg off I did it with the knowledge that it was the only way I could continue to play golf. I was hoping to be able to play each city on the Champions Tour where I would show that life is worth fighting for, no matter what happens. I knew there were zillions of people who didn't know Ken Green, much less the Ken Green story, so my theory was that I was going to help the tour with publicity as well as help out as many people as I could with my story of persistence, while never surrendering to life's asteroids. In my whacked-out head it made perfect sense. I was wrong again.

I'm going to try and explain this as simply as I can without boring you to death. I was playing on the tour with a two-year exemption based on my wins on the regular tour. It was a newish category created because they knew they had screwed some things up. There were guys who had won often on tour but were not exempt on the Champions Tour. Go figure, right? The tour decided to use All Time Dollars as the criteria for exemption. Some of us won our events when the money was relatively small; my first win netted me $81,000, for example. Guys like Tom Pernice and Steve Lowery, who each won a couple of times, are exempt for life because they played well when the money was better. Bobby Wadkins never won on tour yet he was exempt for 13-plus years. So they created my category to give us at least a couple of years, the plan being that if you were good enough to be out there you would play well enough to keep yourself out there. Still wrong, but better than it was, I guess.

In the creation of this category however, they forgot to include a Major Medical amendment. I guess they assumed you would be itching to play through whatever pain you were experiencing, or that nothing bad would ever happen. At the time of the accident that took my leg, I had 14 months left of my exempt status. Clearly I would never be as good as I had been, so that's all I had—14 months.

I decided to use golf, and my trying to help others via golf, as the reason to stay sane. If you have no purpose in life, you're fried. I talked to then Champions Tour president Mike Stevens and he was totally on board with my plan of trying to play each event once. Since they didn't have the Major Medical exemption in my category, I had to ask the tour for a special amendment. Mike told me it was a done deal and the tour was all-in with me. I was really psyched because for the first time in a long time I was playing and fighting on with the sole purpose of helping others and not just me. I would start with one person and work my way up to a million if I could, was my theory.

There was only one hurdle left: the tour had to ask the players to sign off on my medical exemption. Surely this was a no-brainer, right? The shock of my life was about to be delivered to me. The players turned it down. Yes, they said NO.

Wtf, are you kidding me?! I might understand a bunch of 20- or 30-year-olds turning down something like this because they're happy to get rid of one more competitor, not quite understanding what life is really all about. But this was insane. We're all over 50 now and everyone has made their big bucks—and I've got *one leg!* What are they afraid of? Did they not get the real meaning of life, or were they just being selfish dickheads? Sadly, it seems to be both.

The point the players don't get is that they think the Champions Tour means to the fans what the regular tour means. The main reason they think this is because they're trying just as hard now as they did when they were playing the regular tour. What they fail to grasp is that only the die-hard fan cares or watches the golden oldies, as good as they still are.

Here these players had a chance to actually help the many souls whose life had thrown them the asteroid of asteroids: amputees, the disabled, wounded vets, vets, first-responders and others with mental issues, and everyone else who had been thrown a curveball in life. What in God's name did it matter if they added me to the field for a couple of years? Some thought that I wouldn't need the tour exempt status because I would get so many sponsor's exemptions that I could play wherever and whenever I wanted. Unfortunately, for a guy who lost his leg and has brutal pain on a daily basis, it's kind of tricky to plan ahead. Tournaments don't tell you if you're getting an exemption until the week before the tourney, most of the time.

I have never been so pissed and hurt that at our age these guys still don't get what life is all about. How sad for them. Mike Stevens was stunned and so sorry because he knew he had told me it was a done deal, and then he had to tell me that my own peers had taken my missing leg and stuffed it right up my ass. I toyed with suing them but elected not to because this was unlike the PING suit where millions of people were being affected. This was just me and while my intention was to help others less fortunate than I (I am the only player who goes to local hospitals and hosts terminal children at my home I rent for tournaments, at EVERY tournament I attend) I didn't want to sue or hurt the game of golf I love.

So I sucked it up and started writing letters requesting exemptions to all the events. Eight years later and over fifty letters later, I have received one exemption. ONE effing spot. How and why is that even possible? Even if you thought Ken Green was the Dick of Dicks when he was younger, all you had to do was look at what he has said since the accident and how on earth he is handling everything that has been thrown his way.

A couple years after the players told me to shove it, I asked the PGA Tour once again for a medical exemption which would allow me to play the new cities. I thought that this time, once they knew I had received only one exemption in lieu of the dozens they told me I would get, they would clearly see the value of granting me a medical exemption.

So I go through the process once again. I wait patiently as I'm told they have to talk to all the right people and then the players. Once again the tour tells me it's up to the players and yes, once again I got thrown off the cliff with grandma, grandpa and my fake legs. *Holy shit, is this real?* I have no words to describe how I felt. I will never understand why they did this to me, again. I mean these same players donated the pro-am purse two years in a row to help me with my medical expenses. Two hundred thousand dollars, that's a lot of cash, yet they don't think I have any value out there? It was purely optional for each player to give up their potential winnings from the pro-am, and only two, Bob Eastwood and John Daly, said *No, fuck Ken again.* Bob didn't shock me at all, but John surprised me a lot. I guess I should have made him pay me the three thousand he lost to me playing pool in Japan. So after you hear that players donated their pro-am money to my medical bills, why would they still not want me out there giving them much needed PR?

The few events I have played I'm a big part of the show during the week because again, whether I like it or not, it's an unbelievable story. Once this book is out it will be a story all over again. Please understand that not every player voted against me. Mike Reid, my playing partner in the team event, voted with me. Mike Reid is forever in my heart. He wanted to play with me in the Legends of Golf event at a time when this one event could've made the difference in him keeping his card. He was on the bubble so I told him that I'm forever grateful but I understood if he wanted to play with someone else and have a real chance of making big bucks and keeping his card. He looked at me and said, "No way, this is far more important than golf, I'm with you." I will never ever forget that. Mike understood what life's about way earlier than I did- he's been this way for decades. Calc obviously voted my way. But clearly over fifty percent didn't. Yet they all tell me, "No Ken, I voted for you." I can't stand lying, selfish pros. I hope one day you guys figure out what life's really about. Does anyone ask you how many times you've won on the Champions Tour?

The tour sent out their usual PR baloney refuting the boning of Ken Green like any good corporate entity does. I give you my word this was on the players and Finchem. Finchem? I know he doesn't like the Champions Tour but he had the power to overrule the board. He had to have known the value of having me play each event once, but he elected to stay out of it. I'll let you come to your own conclusion. He despises me. *Oops*, my conclusion.

So now I find out I'm screwed over twice by the players and the tour- the organization that prides itself on the "together anything's possible" mantra. Either it's the perfect con job or an incredibly ideal plan. I mean, they give me a couple hundred thousand to help me out with medical costs (I wasn't out buying jet skies with the money) in addition to two private jet rides back from intense surgeries—really great stuff. Then they turn around and stop me dead in my tracks from helping golf and others in need. They kept me from playing their holy grail, the Champions Tour. It just defies logic or common sense. Hell, if they just had the right plan where guys who played the regular tour for 20 years with multiple wins and a Ryder Cup appearance were given some time to play the Champions Tour, this whole morass never happens. I mean, they created a Hall of Fame amendment for foreigners who don't have enough career money to get in normally.

They have tried so many different ways to make sure certain guys are exempt it's scary. I'm just your basic idiot but why wouldn't they just use a system where you get a one-year exemption for each regular tour victory? Then Ben Crenshaw can play till he's 70, instead of now where he's not exempt. *Ben Crenshaw is not exempt on the Champions Tour!!* I mean, would you rather play with Tom Pernice or Ken Green? Ken Green or Ben Crenshaw? It's pretty easy folks, but the egos refuse to acknowledge their tour isn't the regular tour, so you should only have guys who can break 77. The Champions Tour is about promoting golf and helping sponsors dole out fun packages to their clients. It's that simple. But let's just keep guys who haven't had brilliant careers out there who don't say squat to their pro-am partners, and let's keep Fuzzy "never stops talking" Zoeller, and Ken Green, off the golf course. I can ramble on forever but I'm guessing by now even you're sick of listening to me talk about this stupidity.

27/

Honduras 1:
'We will kill your parents'

If I'm telling you the truth I wish I hadn't let this Honduras thing reappear in my brain. After getting back to Connecticut I think I did a good job of blocking it. I just put it in the very back and let it go. But now comes the time when my pain needs to be revealed in an effort to help others.

We had moved to Honduras when I was eleven because my mom felt it might help the family, which was headed by an abusive alcoholic, stay together. She thought a foreign country might help temper my dad's drinking and save their marriage. As a result, my dad took a job as the Principal of The American School in Honduras.

When I got back to Connecticut after those three years away I was a changed person. From an outgoing and gregarious boy I had become a young recluse. I had no friends at all in high school—I didn't trust anyone. I had some golf buddies but I never did anything with them besides play golf. I found peace only on the golf course. I barely got through high school. I thought I had done a great job pushing it to oblivion but writing about it has put it back in my mind. The only time it recedes is when I'm on the golf course and unfortunately my leg and pain won't let me get out there nearly enough damnit.

Maybe I'll have to go see a therapist. Truthfully though, what are they going to tell me that I don't already know? Of course I shouldn't blame myself for what was done. No shit. That's not going to happen though. I do blame myself. How stupid was I for believing the initial reason I was given as a 12-year-old for why we were doing all these things? "Your mom and dad picked me to show you how things work with sex and love," he had said. He said he was honored and felt special for being given this great responsibility. Of course I'm going to blame myself for being so stupid.

I am not sure how a therapist will interpret the fact that I don't hate the man who started it all- my father's 'friend' Louie. I feel sorry for him because he fell into the next trap. He wasn't the one who beat me like a toy and did things that were beyond perverted. He was gentle and he cried, like me. A therapist might tell me I'm not screwed up, that's it's normal to have this whacked-out Stockholm feeling. What the fuck is the matter with me? The nightmare I lived in Honduras may very well have set me up for my fall into depression when things went south with Ellen. It may have prevented me from doing great things on the golf course or in my personal life. It certainly changed my life and it could not have been for the better, so I don't know why I have no bad feelings for the man who began the entire chain of events. I'm almost sixty—I should know better. How did I not see this for what it was when it started, for Pete's sake? How can I look in the mirror and say I don't hate him or have any bad feelings for him? How?

All I know is what I feel. If I didn't fall for his lies the second stage never happens, so how do I not blame the idiot who fell for it? It's me and only me. So I think back now to the second stage when the other two entered the picture. I opened my mouth once about not doing it anymore and got whipped so good I never even thought about trying to speak up again. Then they said they would kill my mother, and again I take the stupid pill. I really believed they would kill her.

Then the real ugly stuff started. How did I not open my mouth and say something? I still wonder. Wtf was wrong with me? And here's the biggest head-scratcher of all: Why did I go back to Honduras that last year? Why didn't I just stay in Connecticut? Well, I know why—they said they would kill my dad. *How dumb was that?* I think now. The look on my mom's face when I told her I wanted to stay with Dad in Honduras still haunts me to this day. A stunned, dull look as tears rolled down her face as she said she understood and would accept my decision. What was wrong with me damnit? Her eyes were there, but not there, if that makes any sense. Is that why I don't look into people's eyes to this day? I don't know.

So I did go back. I guess I figured it couldn't get much worse, maybe. Truth be told I have no clue why I did anything they said. But it wasn't worse—it was *far* worse. The word I'm looking for is "brutal." I still wonder how my Dad never picked up on any of this. Was he that hammered every night? The answer is yes he was, so I guess that's how it happens.

If you're wondering whether how I handled it was right or wrong or justified, all I can tell you today is that I don't think one bit about that. I think only about how stupid I was for falling into the traps. For those of you who feel like pedophiles should be given a second chance or rehabilitation I will tell you all to go fuck yourself. Until you live in the skin of a young soul who was tortured physically, emotionally, and sexually, you have no right to pass judgment on me or assume those no-good souls can be saved. None. The lives of the abused are altered forever and that's just wrong. I will never judge anyone who has done these things because that's not my "job," but in my opinion they should all be killed or thrown into Alcatraz together.

I didn't see me ever telling anyone what happened to me that night, before I fought back. Before I started this book I couldn't see it happening anywhere outside of a therapist's office, but probably not even there. But I am going to tell you and I'm willing to accept judgment for it when it comes time. I just have to figure out how to get these memories out of my head. Maybe telling this story will help toward that goal. It's going to be tricky because I blame myself mostly. I didn't speak up, I was scared, I was young.

If this book and my message resonate with people I clearly need to let it go because I'm hoping to speak to others about all I've gone through in life. It's like I've hit the mega-lottery in reverse. I turned a bright kid with a bright future into a teenage recluse, which was obviously my way of not going nuts or turning into a drug-addicted psycho-maniac. I'm embarrassed to even tell you the thoughts that go through my mind now when I type away, or even at other times. If anyone knew some of the thoughts that go through this head now, you would be stunned, yet they're all clearly from those years and what those years did to me. And while it's maybe all best left unsaid, I am not too smart so I'm going to say it.

I know what happened to me in Honduras wasn't my fault. I know the depression was not my fault. I know the accident and everyone dying wasn't my fault. Yet I'm here to tell you it was my fault. I was in charge of me and those who died. They died on my watch. I have come to terms with it, so don't misunderstand what I'm saying. But they were all my responsibility. Ellen and seven years of court and manipulation of the three kids was her doing and her fault, but it's my fault I fell into depression. Yet I know I had no control over that either. So basically I'm still whacked out. I blame myself for letting her get to Hunter in a small way. I should've seen that she was taking this all the way to hell. I regret not stopping the fighting with Ellen and walking away from Hunter sooner and just taking my chances that he would one day come back to me. Then he might not have been so screwed up by everything that was going on between Ellen and I. The other regret is the fact that Sue and I didn't take Hunter away from Ellen. We had it all planned out. I was quitting golf and we were going overseas when Hunter turned 22. I would let him know his mom and siblings were still alive, and we should have bolted.

28/

Honduras 2:
Soul Destroyed

I guess I was handling the move to the middle of nowhere Tegucigalpa, Honduras, the best any eleven-year-old could. As a kid (just like as an adult) I was a sports nut, but all I had now was soccer. I knew nothing about soccer, Tegucigalpa, or Honduras, damnit. They had some baseball but they wouldn't let me play because Americans weren't allowed to play baseball. I thought it was because we were just way better, but it was actually because they disliked Americans. The next and only other option was golf. So I played golf every day after school. Our house was only half-mile away from the course.

We lived in a big house but it wasn't big enough. My brother had his best friend move down with us so he and Bill shared a room. Sister Shelley had her own room. Then my folks' best friend Louie also moved down, so he had his own room. I had a twin cot in the hallway. I can't say I cared though. I'm 11, so who cares? So all totaled we had seven people plus one maid, Kia. I didn't know it at the time but Kia would one day become my Honduran mom.

At some point in that first year I began waking up without my pajamas on. I had no clue how it happened, I just figured I was a wingnut and my PJ's just had a way of coming off each night. Then one night I woke up and there was Louie, playing with me. I was confused.

But my confusion wouldn't last long because Louie was very helpful in educating me about why he was touching me while I slept. He said that every parent chooses a good friend to help their child learn about sex and their body. Louie said he would show me how to do things that I would like and enjoy. He said he was honored that they choose him for this job. He said sex is a hush-hush subject so we could never say anything to anyone. He had been a close friend of my parents forever so I just thought it was all fine. I mean, this is 1970 and there's no real TV or media in Honduras and certainly no internet or social media. I was a clueless little boy.

The days and weeks and months passed. We had our 'love sessions' and I thought it was all completely normal. I can't believe I was that naive. The first year passed and we lost Bill's friend from home to graduation. We now also lived in a different home. Again, this home was big, but I still got stuck in the hall on a cot. Funny how my sleeping in a common area (without a door to lock) was the one constant, despite the fact we had lots of space.

The second year things would change for the worse. Louie was still doing his thing with me but I never really gave it much thought. Somewhere towards the middle of that second year however, he brought a couple of his 'friends' into the mix. They soon became my new friends. My love lessons now included two additional participants. I don't really recall what I thought but I do know it was different. We were now doing things that were way, way different and I didn't quite get it or like it because it was getting physical and way, way more perverted and ugly. I'm not sure I knew how it was worse but I was aware things were much more intense and we were doing things that even as a 12-year-old I knew were just dead wrong. Louie was different too. He was quiet as they ran the show and the 'lessons.'

They didn't always arrive together, and we were doing it in new places. These days it was always in outside locations. Then one time it started to get very physical. I was scared to death and had no idea what to do. Why was this happening? Why was I getting hit and beaten when I was doing everything I was supposed to be doing?

Then near the end of the second year I just said I'm not doing this anymore. I told them I wasn't going to do this anymore and I was going to tell my dad. I was then beaten harder than ever before and had to lie to my mom when welts appeared. When I stopped crying I was told that if I ever said anything they would kill my mother. I believed them one hundred percent. I have no idea how I believed it, but I did. More time passed and the abuse continued. Then it happened.

My dad was a big-time alcoholic and my folks had moved to Honduras to try and save their marriage. But after two years my mom had made the decision that the marriage was doomed and she was going back to Connecticut with her kids. I had no idea that this decision had been reached. One day shortly thereafter, after a particularly grueling session where I was humiliated and ganged up on, they told me my mom was going to leave but that I had to tell her I wanted to stay with my dad. Again, I was told they would kill my dad. I don't know how I believed them, but I did. I mean, I was getting beaten regularly so the idea that they would do the same, and worse, to my parents, was a no-brainer. I didn't know what else to believe. I was scared to death, not just for me but for my dad. The fact that my abusers knew about all this family business before I did only reinforced my notion that I should trust these people.

Then Mom came to me. She explained it was time to go home. Dad was going to stay with Louie. We were going home. What I said next haunts me to this day. I told Mom I wanted to stay. I'll never ever forget the look in her eyes. I had crushed her. She was crying but said nothing. She then told me it was okay, that she understood. I wanted to scream but I said nothing, I just froze. I was so sure they were going to kill my father. So my mom left and I was about to have the worst experience of my life.

THE END OF THE BEGINNING

That year the four of us; Louie, my dad and I, and our maid Kia, lived on top of Allateo Mountain. It was one scary, sharp-curved drive up and down the mountain. It made the mountainside roads of Italy look like 5-lane Sacramento freeways. These were half-paved curvy-ass turns with straight drops-of-death waiting around each corner.

Dad decided to give me the master bedroom in seeming compensation for two years of hall-monitor duty. The room had its own porch, which would turn out to be more like a suite-adjacent torture chamber. Without my mom there to kind of guard me I was now doomed. My dad's drinking got worse. They were over all the time now. It seemed like they were there every other night and always on the weekends. I finally figured out that when Dad passed out I was in deep trouble. I used to try everything to keep him awake. I used to wonder why he never woke up, not knowing what alcohol did to you. The sex, or whatever it was, started to get even more ugly. It was disgusting what was happening, and how it was happening. I was getting beaten every other day while they were laughing and having their way with me. I was slowly dying.

Kia used to come to my room after it was all over and I would just cry and cry and cry while she held me. *How did my Dad not know?* I would wonder.

One day I arrived at school a little late. As I approached the school a teacher rushed up to me with a concerned look on her face. She shuffled me off to an empty room to keep something from me. But it was too late- I had seen them. At some point somebody had flyers printed up. The flyers said that my dad and Louie and others were having orgies and things. I remember all the kids were brought up to the auditorium to discuss this. I wanted to scream but couldn't do a thing. I have no idea what was said or if anything was determined or resolved, I just remember wanting to scream.

I'm now a shell. I had been a very outgoing kid, one who excelled in all sports. Now I said nothing and I did nothing. Nothing but play golf. The course was my heaven and my haven. I would play all day long while they drank up a storm, knowing I was doomed the moment I returned home.

The year was coming to an end, and whether that played into the brutality of this particular night, I can't say for sure. But it was a particularly brutal night. Only one of them was there and they were having a drunkfest of drunkfests. Then Dad went down for the count.

I'm not going to go into detail here about what happened to me that night because it's just so disgusting and gross, but you can read more about it at the end of this book. It's beyond imagination. I will say that Kia had to free me and clean me off. He had forgotten to clean me up in his drunken stupor, I guess. I don't even know if I said anything to Kia. I have no idea how late it was, I was just there, floating in a surreal existence.

I remember Dad telling me this before I got onto the plane: "Kid, I'm sorry. You did nothing wrong. Don't ever tell anyone, ever."

Since I allowed this back into my head I keep asking myself how I fell for this? Why didn't I say anything to anyone? How could I have been so stupid?

I actually don't hate Louie. How do I not hate him?! What he did is awful, yet why don't I hate him? I don't get that. He was a prisoner too, but it would've never happened without him, *but I don't hate him*. How stupid of me. As for the man in my bed, I don't give a flying flip about him. He destroyed the *me* I was supposed to be.

29/

What Now?

So now I'm me again and I realize much of the pain I have caused without knowing it at the time. I destroyed a beautiful relationship with Sue and her son Joey. Lord knows why some of my friends didn't tell me to go bang a brick. I have no recollection of how I was as a friend during those 2-3 years. I ruined a career when I was starting to go full tilt. I occasionally wonder how many times I would've won if I hadn't fallen apart. All I know is it was a living nightmare. I mean, how many people can say their dog is the only reason they are breathing fresh air instead of sucking on ashes. So being human-Ken again is great but I will always have to pay attention to the symptoms of depression until I die. I've had a few times where I had to up my dosage in the past eight years due to all the dramatic occurrences and emotional pain I've gone through, but it's amazing how once you know what to look for you can see your way back when previously that path was never even on my radar in the slightest. Thirty-plus million Americans are in some type of depression, and I urge everyone to learn the symptoms because I promise you know someone who is struggling through it. That's way too many people who are basically walking zombies without the ugly faces- well maybe some do have those faces.

So I'm an old goat and you're wondering how does a soul recover from so many dramatic events in one's life. The early physical and sexual abuse, depression, loss of wife and brother, the loss of your leg and your livelihood, and then your son dies. Damn, if they made a movie you might think it's complete bull. No way all that can happen to one guy. Plus, he was one of the best golfers on earth to boot.

Well, I blocked the early days with pretty good results, unless you count the unknown damage done to me, which of course we will never know. Maybe the fall into depression was because of Honduras. Seven years of fights in court with your ex can do it too. I promise you I've tried not to bash her and I'm sorry if some feel I've done that but I'm only trying to explain how and why I fell into depression. I did, and in the end it's my fault for not being strong enough. So more years pass and just when life is going great the asteroid of all asteroids hits me. Jeannie and Billy are dead. Nip, my precious 24/7 dog, is dead. My leg is playing gator bait and my golf career and second chance is dead.

I swore to myself I would never fall into depression again, so failure was not an option. Then your baby boy, whom you had finally reconnected with the past few years, is found dead. So you just say screw it and die like so many of my friends thought I might? Bullshit. *It's a simple plan of attack*, I thought. Use this as your purpose and reason to live. Don't let life's tragedies win. I mean, if you're an atheist and this happens to you, you're screwed right? So you're going to be pure ashes in thirty years or you can join the ash world now. So you either fight life with the remaining years you have left on earth and live them to the fullest or kill yourself out of depression or drink yourself into oblivion. It's tough to be an atheist, I'm telling you. So now you think you're a religious soul. Then the mega asteroid hits you. Do you just live life in a dull state of blah or do you trust that the Big Guy will take care of you when it's all done. It's hard, right? And of course the old question arises: If God was good why would he do all this? My belief is simple, like me. We have free will, and life happens with happiness and ugliness. We learn from all and those who learn faster, grow more. We love all and those who learn to love all, grow faster. I've learned not to be angry with Ellen- I forgave her years ago. I'm trying to forgive myself, which is the hardest thing to do. That being said, I refuse to not fight on and do all I can. If I help one person that's enough, but I'm hoping for two or more. We are all different. We all do things our way. Just don't give up is all I'm asking.

Every time I think about Honduras I keep thinking the same thing over and over. How could I have been so dumb and believed what I was told? I know it's not my fault but I blame myself. It's no different than Jeannie or Billy and the RV accident. I know it wasn't my fault but they were my responsibility. Honduras is worse, and harder, I think. What will my friends think of me when they find out? Will I lose any friends? Will they be afraid to tell their dopey jokes or will they just stroll away? When will I lose that demon of blame that goes off in my head every time I talk about this story?

I have to get beyond it, I do. Because only then will I be able to help those other victims so they can let it out before their life goes up in flames. I was lucky, so very luck, that my life didn't plunge into Suck City after Honduras. I know it was because of golf. Other kids might not have golf though, so I'm going to try and be their golf. One kid at a time.

- Ken Green

ADDENDUM/

The Really Ugly Truth
About My Sexual Abuse

I've gone back and forth as to whether I explain to the world how brutal my stories of sexual and physical abuse were. I'm not sure anyone wants to read about some of the torturous episodes that went on. However, if I don't go into detail, will people do what they've been doing for centuries and just forget about it? It's easy to say, 'Wow that's horrible,' and move on, filling in the blanks (or not) yourself- perhaps telling yourself that these were maybe little acts of indiscretion or perversion. Like anything else, there are different levels of abuse and if I don't detail mine, how can I get anyone to change some of our weak State laws involving pedophilia? States like Vermont and Hawaii are just ridiculous in terms of how lenient they are to these dark souls.

At first I felt that there was no way in hell I could detail publicly some of the things that were done to me as a child. Never. There was no way I was going to tell my friends and others what was done to me or I what I was forced to do. But after letting this thought percolate for several months, I believe that if I don't detail these acts maybe nothing will change. I've elected to let each one of you know some of the ugly details with the hope that we, or you, can start the ball rolling to help reduce the number of sexually abused kids in our world.

Of course, even if I do go into detail, there is a good chance that nothing will change, and then I'm out in the open for the world to see and I will be forced to relive my terror for the rest of my life, for no good reason other than my good intentions- which in the end, may be all I can fall back on- *good intentions*.

I'm petrified I'm going to lose some friends after this book comes out. They will still be *friends,* but will they be scared about how they think and act around me? Will *they* be the same? I hope most will, but it's scary.

Then there's my inability not to blame myself, thinking I'm some loser for not opening my mouth. I get the sentiment *'It's not your fault, you did nothing wrong,'* but I promise you, most of us feel like idiots. When I decided to write my book of the Good, the Bad and the Ugly, the #MeToo movement had not yet come to life. The Nassar, Weinstein and other ugly souls were not in the news yet. I'm thinking their stories and others have played a role in my decision to reveal how ugly these things get. Now must just be the time to let people know how god-awful things do get in this world. Every abuse is horrific, but I'm afraid we don't ever understand how bad some are. I pray mine was rare as can be, but I truthfully have no clue. I'm going to explain a few of the things that happened, *and only a few*, so I'm sure you will get a new understanding of sexual abuse. Lord knows what the mental abuse does to all of us. Maybe it can help change your State's laws.

<u>WARNING: GRAPHIC DETAILS OF</u>
<u>SEXUAL ABUSE AND RAPE TO FOLLOW</u>

The early days with just Louie was what I now would call 'normal sex stuff' with no physical beatings and just sex. Yes, it's still dead wrong, but I would've given anything to just have had that.

That said, please know you're about to walk into the world I lived as a pre-teenager, and I would ask you to envision yourself in my shoes at age 11, 12 and 13. Then you may begin to understand this nasty world of sick human beings.

***

I had to learn very fast when they played their games, one of which was Beat the Clock. This was the game where if the grown men didn't ejaculate by a certain time, I was beaten. They would laugh while I did what I had to do to finish them off. It would depend on their mood as to how much time I was given. They laughed and laughed as I did what I did, trying to avoid getting my ass whooped.

When there are two grown men taking and doing things to a young boy, things that only the darkest souls can manage, I'll just let you imagine what was done. I wasn't a willing partner in these threesomes. It was not a one-at-a-time scenario. It was hard-core, two sickos having violent sex with a young boy. It's a disgusting, grotesque picture of abuse, force, and torture.

But even that wasn't enough. They developed intricate games combined with different locations and positions. I was just a toy, a defenseless little boy who was treated like a ragdoll sex toy. I was their One Act boy who had to dress up and perform as they wanted. *'Why did I get a beating when I did just as they told me they wanted?'* I always asked myself after it was over. *Why?*

I'm clueless as to whether I'm making you see the picture without having to spell it all out. Truth is, I have no idea how often this happened, except to say to me it seemed daily.

I'm going to try to explain in detail the last night anything happened. Why would I do this? I'm not sure.

It was just him and me. My outside 'torture-porch,' where most of this always happened was, I guess, your basic porch. It was lined with a rock wall and flower beds. This evening I was tied down against the brick wall and I will tell you that every damn time he pounded me from behind he shoved my face into the dirt. Time after time I was eating and choking on dirt. I could care less about what he was doing back there, but I couldn't breathe. I was choking and eating dirt. Try to envision a full-grown adult doing that to a terrified young kid who couldn't do anything right in their eyes, yet I did everything they wanted. I thought I was dying. Then he finished and just left. He just left me there. I couldn't move.

The housekeeper Kia, who was really my surrogate mother after my own mom had left to go back to the States, eventually came to my rescue. She untied me and cleaned off my bloodied body from the rocks I was jammed into. I was my usual self; detached and crying. She took me to her room and I just sat there as she cleaned and patched me up.

After a while I left her room and went back to my porch to go to my bed. I went into my room and *THERE HE WAS!* He was sleeping in my bed! My rapist was sleeping soundly in his victim's little bed.

I went outside and picked up a good-sized rock and brought it back to my room. And then I hit him with the rock as hard and for as long as I could muster the strength. I have no idea what I felt then, but I know what I feel now. Pain.

I then ran to my father's room and told him what happened. He and Louie took over from there and my Dad swore me to secrecy. I don't know what happened to the guy. They put me on the next plane back to the United States and we never talked about it again.

I've told no one else over the years.

Until you.

LET IT FLY

The Uncommon World Of Ken Green

=== By Tim Rosaforte ===

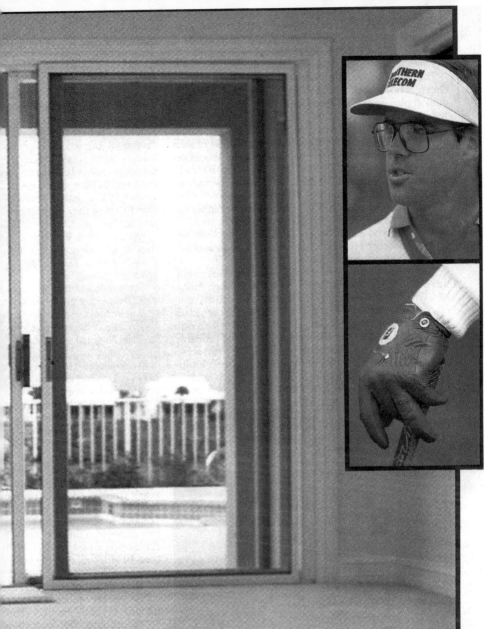

iding glass doors were open, and Green had a 3-wood with a black hite shaft in his hands. A new golf was sitting on his living room car- uld have been the second shot to a as by no means a set-up shot, a ng to show off. "I've emptied three rough this door," Green says.

d echoes off the walls. The ball flies swimming pool and the seventh ear Lakes CC in West Palm Beach, lly splashing into a pond short of e. Green looks disappointed.

"Bunted that one," he says, tapping another ball into place. He eyes the space between the glass doors, and his target some 240 yards away. He could almost do this blindfolded. He was conducting an interview between shots.

Thwack!

This ball landed on the bank in front of the tee. Green posed on it.

"Ooooooo," he says. "Got that baby over. Someone will pick that bad boy up."

There's never a bad lie on this tee box, no gouge marks in the carpet. This is a game that started one night when Bear Lakes member Bill Torrey was over. After a few beers, Green had closed the sliding glass doors down to about 12 inches apart, and was firing 4-irons through the opening for Torrey, the New York Islanders general manager. Thwack!

This one lands on the white tees. A perfect shot. Green, who won three tournaments and more than $1 million playing golf worldwide in 1988, flushed it. "That was probably 240," he says. "Full bore."

Even back when he was grinding and slashing, when he couldn't have paid for the windows if he had broken them—and he says he never has—Ken Green would do things like stand on a hotel bed and take $5 at 100-to-1 odds from a friend that he could hit a 5-iron through a window and land it on a tent 170 yards away.

The friend paid Green $500. Green bought dinner the rest of the week. "Hitting it off a bed's a harder shot," says Green, who started by chipping balls into sinks before graduating to middle irons off the mattress and 3-woods through the sliding glass doors.

You wouldn't see somebody like Jack Nicklaus trying this out his back door in nearby Lost Tree Village. But Ken Green is no traditionalist. He may have grown up on the New England border, but his style is more urban New York than upstate Connecticut. He says what's on his mind and goes after par-five greens that he probably shouldn't. He throws his putter at his caddie in an act that's become a sideshow. He comes in the press room at the Nabisco Championships, at Pebble Beach, and jokes about how it's been two weeks since he's seen his wife Ellen, and how horny he is.

Green would never stay at the Lodge at Pebble Beach, not at $250 a night. He feels that's a rip off. He also rips the condition of the course, commenting on how it's gone downhill since Marvin Davis took over.

Green says that rather than putting money back in golf course, Davis is putting it in his pocket.

All this after shooting 67 in an opening round w he only hit seven fairways. He was three back of C Strange, and he says, "I've got to play better to co with Curtis or Joe Blow, whoever is up there. I've get to the range and find out what it is. If I don't, shit out of luck."

A lot of people find some of his actions and wo distasteful, but who are they to say? They're the es lishment, and Green is not. They might talk like th the locker room or the men's grill, but never in a conference. They would never give the middle-fin gesture to their ball, as Green did during the 1982 dian Open. If they threw a club, it would be out o ger, not fun.

"As far as how the other players perceive me, I' they don't understand me. They probably don't vi the way I am as being right," Green says. "But the spect my golfing ability."

Green just acts like he's on a softball field. He's jock. Don Mattingly might say "shit" and throw his ting helmet after striking out, but he's at home pla the middle of Yankee Stadium, not the ninth green Augusta National.

"He could handle things a little more tastefully," Ben Crenshaw. "He's an exciting player, but to be honest, a person like me, who is a traditionalist, ca condone his actions.

"Ken sees things a little differently. He's even sai an anti-hero. That's something he'll have to live do for a long time. You don't have to be a conformist anything like that, but after all, golf's supposed to l gentlemen's game."

Golf has its share of hypocrisy, and if Green is su bad guy, why was he the third player picked at this year's Tournament of Champions pro-am (behind nold Palmer and Greg Norman)? And why has a bi poration like Northern Telecom signed him to a lu tive three-year contract? And why has he only been fined once, a measly $250 when a woman sent six onds of video tape to the PGA Tour, showing Gree gering the missed putt at the Canadian Open?

"He's not a monster," said Crenshaw.

"He's never bothered me, and I've seen the same things everybody else has seen," said Strange.

"I don't agree with everything Ken Green says or does, but I think Ken Green is just being himself," Mark McCumber. "If he feels he needs to change, it to him. I don't think he has any malicious intent w he says some of the things he does. So the questio does Ken Green like the perception of himself? If h doesn't, he can change it."

Does Ken Green like the perception of himself? I must, because he's not doing anything differently n than when he was a nobody. "I don't think I've cha much," he says. "I'm just playing better and more p ple see me. I used to throw clubs at Shelley (his sis and former caddie), not as hard as I do at Joe (LaCa But people didn't care then because I wasn't any go

"What I say just comes out. If I sat and thought a

WILL HERTZBERG

of the things I say, I wouldn't say them. But that's
y style. My feeling is, if I don't just talk like I talk,
wouldn't be me and that's no good, either."
en has never had any complaints at being mis-
d. He does have problems with context. When he
about being horny at Pebble Beach, he figured it
never leave the press room and appear in print.

en went as far as explaining it had been a little
month since Ellen delivered newborn son Hunt-
d Green had spent the past two weeks on the
It came out like he was crude, when he was actu-
eing cute.
x is an everyday occurence," Green says. "People
o have sex. You can make fun of it."
en makes fun of just about everything. He's al-
goofing on somebody, including himself, and the
leaves his interviews with notebooks full of good
ial. The buzzwords are that the tour lacks color.
reen is color, right down to his trademark glove.
if some of what he says is blue, it's usually true.
major goal of mine is not to change," he says.
le are always telling me I'm supposed to play the
. They say I should mislead people and not say
s on my mind."
e, for example, at this year's Los Angeles Open, a
e on Green appeared in the *Los Angeles Times* en-
"The Color of Money." In it, Green was outspoken
comments Arnold Palmer had made regarding
American players lacking heart ("That's a
.") and about the majors being overstated
y're figments of Jack's and the media's
nation.").
reaction from many players was that Green was
like it is. "But they just won't get into it," says
. Whether it be his 7-degree driver off a tight fair-
e, or at a member of the tight-lipped establish-
Green will let it fly.

At Westchester, where he lost a playoff to Seve Ballesteros, he was asked if it was intimidating playing with
Seve and Greg Norman. Green shrugged, "My feeling is
they'll see just as much good golf watching me as I will
watching them."
Westchester and Hartford, since they are closest to his
Connecticut home, are Green's majors. Victories at
Doral and the Honda Classic would complete his local
grand slam. "The media make major tournaments, not
the players." he said before this year's Honda tournament. "For example, you couldn't find a much better
field than there was at Doral. Today, players are left out
of so-called majors who have the ability to win. Percent-
age-wise, it makes it easier for players who are there."
Green made headlines last year at Greensboro, not so
much for losing a playoff to Sandy Lyle, but for losing it
on the Masters Committee. If he won Greensboro—and
he had a one-stroke lead before three-putting the 72nd
hole—Green would have been at Augusta National. Instead, he flew home to West Palm Beach.
"I'm a little amazed people treat it as 'the place,'" he
said at the time. "The design of the greens is ridiculous.
It always amazed me. The top players criticized the
greens at the TPC when it was a baby. Augusta is the
same way, but nobody criticizes it. They say it's a great
place. I never quite figured it out. But I'll give them all
the credit in the world for pulling off the scam they do.
"I don't care for the people at Augusta and they do
not care for me," Green says. "But I would love to win
the Masters. I don't agree with their policies, but you'd
have to be a fool not to wih the Masters."
You'd have to be a fool to believe that Ken Green is
going to go away. This is not somebody who came up
with everything handed to him. He learned to play the
game at Richter Park, a public course, near his home-
town of Danbury, Conn. In the winter, he would wrap
black tape around a plastic golf ball and play in the
snow around his apartment complex. In the summer, he
would work on his short game under the street lights at
Richter. In school, he would sit in the back of the class
and draw imaginary golf holes and layouts.
When he got his driver's license, Green would drive
the back roads across the New York state border to an
exclusive course in Brewster. He would park on a dirt
road, and sneak on the course with his German Shepherd, Nip. "I never worried about getting caught,"
Green says. But one night, he returned to his car and
found a flat tire. As he was changing it, the superinten-
drove up, screaming at Green. Nip came barking to his
owner's rescue. "I'll never forget the look on that guy's
face," Green says. "He's yelling at me through his truck
window. I'm sitting there, laughing at him."
Until he got together with instructor Peter Kostis in
1984, Green was a self-made golfer. He still is a self-
made man. His only two close friends on tour are Bill
Sander and Mark Calcavecchia, guys he played the mini-
tours with. At home, he spends nearly all his time with
his family. For recreation, he'll drink beer and play full-
contact ping pong with a big, bearded friend, Eric Larson, putting dents in his walls diving for shots. It's not
like he's calling up Greg Norman to meet out at the

like he's calling up Greg Norman to meet at Lost Tree mansion.

"Obviously I care how people perceive him," Ellen Green says. "Somebody you love, you want people to see him as you do. You want people to think your kid is neat, because you think he's neat."

Ken is still a kid, and not a neat one, at heart. The playroom in their new house is going to be nearly 1,220 square feet. Ellen explains that her husband wants a place where he and Brad, their oldest son, can play ball without crashing into lamps.

He's always playing a game, always competing. He doesn't let Brad win, just as he doesn't let Larson win at ping pong, or Calcavecchia at bowling or billiards. According to Ellen, there's not a real separation between his adult and child activities, and daughter Brooke "is as tough as nails" because of it. She also says he can "make a mess as good as any kid."

"He's incredibly successful, yet it hasn't gone to his head at all," Ellen says. "When he has a party, everybody from the bag room guys to th John Linstroths (former president c Bear Lakes) of the world come and meet. I think that's something abou Kenny that's really admirable. He just doesn't judge people. He takes people for what they are. Just think he made a million three last year, and he doesn't put on any airs. He doesn't expect to be treated any be ter or any worse. He's just a real pe son. Money doesn't change him. Success doesn't change him."

There are sides to Ken Green not many people see. He just bought a portable phone that can be used in all 50 states. He keeps it in his golf bag so he can call home in the mid dle of his rounds.

Ellen also bought two fax machines, one Ken can take on the road so the children can send crayon drawings to their father when he's away, and so he can send rhymes home to them. Their average monthly phone bill is $600.

"These are the things that matter, Ellen says.

It is because of his family that Ke Green played in the $1 million chal lenge in Sun City at the end of 1988 He has been criticized for it, but many of the big names have played in Bopthuswana before.

"I'm not Ben Crenshaw, I'm not ultra nice," Green says. "But I don't consider myself a rebel. I have no causes. It's just me."

The phone rings at Ken Green's house, and a recorder answers:

"We all wonder who indeed is th best. I've studied hard, all the boys from East to West. There could be a case for a chap named Lyle...we'll just have to wait a while. My friend Mark swings a pretty good stick, bu I'm sorry to say he's not my pick. Most would say it's the man from Spain, I personally think they're all insane. Some might say that it's eve me, on that we'll just have to wait and see. But now I'm off to the range, to try and catch Mr. Strange."

Beeeeeeeep.

This is not a message many tour players would leave, but if you don know that by now, you've missed the point. Ken Green is not a typical tour player, and if you don't like it, tough s_ _ _ _. ●

IT'S NOT EASY BEING KEN GREEN

by Patrick Leahy

As a confused teenager, living in assorted outposts like Tegucigalpa, Honduras; an Indian reservation in northeastern Arizona; and even Danbury, Conn., young Ken Green held no other thoughts but to play professional golf someday. Today, at the age of 28, that early insatiable passion for the game of golf has pushed him to the brink of stardom on the PGA TOUR.

"It's been my dream, my only dream, since I was 15 years old," recalled Green, who earlier this summer surprised almost everyone by winning the much-ballyhooed and richly-endowed International tournament at the Castle Pines Golf Club, south of Denver. "Even though I wasn't any good as a young player, I still had that dream."

His singleness of purpose wasn't always greeted with unbridled enthusiasm by the people who loved him. His father (Martin), an educator, naturally encouraged the lad to take his studies more seriously.

"I hated school," confessed Green, who left Nonnewaug High School in Woodbury, Conn., when authorities wouldn't let him play varsity golf because he hadn't logged enough time in the classroom. His subsequent matriculation to New Milford High School lasted all of one day. He didn't like it there either, so he quit. Another time, he visited his father who by that time was teaching at an Indian school in Arizona. In three months, he attended classes three times.

"I remember the day I told my Mom 'I'm gonna be a professional golfer'. She was stunned and very skeptical at first, but without her support, I never would have made it."

Although born in Danbury, Conn., Ken did not learn about golf until the age of 12 when his family moved to Honduras for three years (1970-72) while his father was serving as the principal of the American School there.

In restrospect, Ken became a golfer almost by default. His athletic choices were limited. He wasn't good enough to play soccer; because he was American, he wasn't allowed to compete in baseball, so he took up golf. He learned the rudiments of the game on a nine-hole course called the Tegucigalpa Country Club. Among the first things he learned was to keep his head down, his eyes on the ball and not to pay attention to the naked peasant women washing clothes in the river that ran alongside the course. Some lessons were harder than others.

In 1971, Ken had progressed to where he was asked to represent Honduras in the Central American Junior Championships in Managua, Nicaragua. He found out he had a lot to learn.

When his parents split up, Ken returned to the United States with his mother.

"My mom worked two, three jobs, as an accountant, a waitress, a barmaid, the gamut, so that I would not have to work. She let me chase my dream of becoming a professional golfer. She also saved up the money that helped me get started on the mini-tour.

"All this time, Mom rarely got more than one to four hours of sleep per night, but her faith in me never died. There's no one on this earth whom I admire more than my Mom. I'll be forever thankful."

Green's golf habits drove local country club people crazy because he would sneak over fences and practice to his heart's content on their private preserves without their permission.

"I got kicked off golf courses about 800 times," laughed Green. "I figured they wouldn't throw a kid in jail so I just kept doing it."

Most club members nicely looked the other way, but others downright resented his trespasses against them and would kick him off. It didn't stop him. Rigdewood Country Club in Danbury, where Green was a caddie, went so far as to suspend him in 1975.

Green is now a feature player on the PGA TOUR. He has won two TOUR titles, including the 1985 Buick Open and the 1986 International. Guess what? He's still jumping the back fences. As recently as a few months ago, Ken was still sneaking on the back holes at Ridgewood.

It's not easy being (Ken) Green.
Ken did finally blend into the High School scene in his junior year at Danbury high school. He was a member of the golf team that finished second to Staples of Westport in the state high school championship.

As a senior, Ken went undefeated in seven matches and posted a 68 at one of his favorite golf courses Richter Park. (*Golf Digest* rates Richter Park as one of the top 10 public courses in the country.) But an injury to his left wrist required surgery in May of 1976 and he missed the balance of the season. One year later, at Palm Beach Junior College, he needed a second operation that kept him out of action for seven months.

Injuries stalked him. He developed a rotater cuff problem in his right shoulder that kept him off the mini-tour for another seven months in 1981. His doctor recommended cortisone treatments and special exercises, and gradually the condition cleared up.

"Apparently, I have a bad skeleton, in other words, a poorly jointed body," Green explained. "This year, my wrist and shoulder problems sidelined me for two weeks.

"My wrist can't stand the pounding. It's curbed my practice time. Whereas I might hit 200 practice balls, I'm limited to 100 and I'll pace myself. I very seldom play more than four events in a row."

Despite his physical miseries, Ken does not necessarily shy away from other recreational sports. He's a very good bowler and he and close friend Mark Calcavecchia bowl often in the evening. Ken maintains a 200 average and has bowled a 275 game.

When Ken was recovering from the second wrist operation in college, he took up pocket billiards. He's become a skilled enough pool shark to run 84 balls.

At one time, he was an avid

tennis player, but he can't play now because of the shoulder. Instead, he plays platform tennis. The shoulder hurts only when he serves.

It's not easy being (Ken) Green.
Green doesn't feel comfortable about basking in his current glory. He isn't sure he has convinced skep-

Ken, with sister Shelly, en route to winning The International at Castle Pines Golf Club, just outside of Denver.

...s who didn't think he would make in big-time professional golf.

"I'll always have my doubters," ...dmits Green, who is really a very ...kable everyday kind of guy. "Some ...ought the Buick victory was a ...uke, but now that I've won twice, I ...el I don't have anything to prove to ...nyone anymore."

It's been one long uphill strug-...le for respectability. After his high ...chool ordeal, Green headed south ...r Palm Beach Junior College ...here his game began to blossom. ...lis play was noticed by the Univer-...ity of Florida golf coach, who re-...ruited him for the 1978-79 season. ...en's teammates included Calca-...ecchia and Larry Rinker.

His last two summers of ama-...eur golf boosted his confidence ...urther. In 1978 he and John Par-...ons took the Ike Team Champion-...hip. He won the 1979 Azalea Ama-...eur, took second low amateur in ...he 1979 Met Open, finished fourth ...n the Porter Cup and seventh in the ...Northeast Amateur.

Ken turned professional later ...hat year and eventually won four ...nini-tour events, but he was only ...narking time until he earned his ...ᵖGA TOUR privileges. At long last, ...ie earned his TOUR card in the fall ...of 1981, but he lost it right back ...vhen he earned only $11,899 in ...982.

Ken re-qualified, then cracked ...he top 125 in 1983 by winning ...i40,263. He slumped again in 1984 ...o only $20,160 and was forced to ...e-qualify again.

In November of 1984, Green ...ought help of noted golf instructor, ...ᵖeter Kostis. On Green's overall ap-...proach to the game: "Ken is a very ...ᵍood putter. He's a very smart play-...ᵉr. He's put in a lot of work on his ...ᵍame. He's got the desire to be-...come a consistent winner on the ...ᵀOUR. And he's got all the confi-...ᵈence in the world," said Kostis.

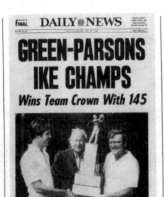

FINAL DAILY⊛NEWS

GREEN-PARSONS IKE CHAMPS

Wins Team Crown With 145

Ken made the front page of the *Daily News* with his Ike Team victory.

His first three years on the PGA TOUR, Ken was sponsored by a syndicate, i.e., a group of backers, organized by his uncle Jack.

"I lost my sponsors because my uncle didn't feel comfortable asking his friends for more money," Green explained. "I certainly understood their position. I simply wasn't playing very well."

When his cash reserve ran low in the first half of the 1985 season, Green thought about leaving the TOUR. He had decided not to enter the Heritage Classic at Hilton Head. A friend named Colonel Gaddy staked him to some money that enabled him to make one last three-tournament swing. It was a godsend.

At the Heritage, Ken tied for 20th and won $4,500, then on to Texas where he finished 11th in the Houston Open and tied for 23rd in the Byron Nelson Classic. More good performances followed, then came the breakthrough at the Buick Open.

It's not easy being (Ken) Green.

His sudden prosperity did not guarantee happiness in his per-sonal life. Ken is the father of a five-year-old son, Ken Jr., from a marriage that ended last year. Ken shares joint custody with his ex-wife Savera. Kenny traveled with his dad on TOUR for a few events this past summer.

"Life on the TOUR is very hard, especially when you are travelling with a small baby and are low on funds," said Green of the breakup.

"That't why I'm so fortunate to have my sister Shelley as my caddie on tour. She helps me deal with the loneliness out there. She's my confidant and my best friend. I can say things to her that nobody else could say to their caddie.

"If not for Shelley, I might have already remarried and been divorced again. Some guys go from one bad marriage to the next. That's the way it is out here."

It's not easy being (Ken) Green.

Ken continues to play out of the Watertown Country Club. He is very proud of his ties to the nutmeg state and that his Buick Open victory was the first PGA TOUR title by a Connecticut live-in resident.

Winning the 1985 Connecticut Open ranks among his proudest achievements. His four-under-par 209 total at the New Haven Country Club earned him a seven-stroke winning margin.

"I never had an opportunity to play in the Connecticut State Amateur because I could never work out my schedule, but I want to be able to say 'I won my State Open'.

"I'd also like to win the Canon Sammy Davis Jr. Greater Hartford Open because it is the only regular TOUR event in my home state. It's a great thrill to walk up the 18th fairway at the TPC of Connecticut and to hear the ovation that tens of thousands of fans give all the players. It's the closest thing that could bring me to tears on a golf course."

HE'S ALREADY BEGUN TO CONTRIBUTE SOMETHING BACK. KEN HAS ORGANIZED A CHARITY PRO-AM AT RICHTER PARK.

It's not easy being (Ken) Green.
Even as he peaked in the 1985 Buick Open, Green soon would hit another dry spell that continued into 1986. Earlier this year, he missed eight cuts, including three in a row right before the International.

That's when his mom swung into action. Jane got in touch with a tarot card lady, in Katonah, N.Y., who had predicted his Buick victory the year before. What did the fates have in store for Ken, she wanted to know?

The lady told her: "Tell Kenny not to worry. He's going out west to a new place, a different place. He's going to win a major tournament with lots of money, and he'll beat a fellow with blonde hair."

"There I was, in the final round of a $1 million tournament, and suddenly the tarot lady's prediction hit me," said Green. "I'm shooting 66 on a new golf course in the Rocky Mountain foothills, and my closest challenger was a blonde West German named Bernhard Langer. It gave me an eerie feeling." Coincidentally, Green's Buick and International victories came on the same tournament dates one year apart.

Green's six birdie, no-bogey 66 earned him $180,000 for winning the debut of one of the few $1 million events in professional golf.

"I'm not up in the heat like this very often. And I haven't contended that much. But something seemed to click out there. I wanted to win. Other times, I'm hacking and choking.

"I haven't had the greatest career, but I can play, maybe not as well as Jack Nicklaus, but I can still play. I was really determined to win out there."

It's not easy being (Ken) Green.
Ken's mom had one other occasion to call on the tarot card lady. In October of 1985, a few months after the Buick Open, the lady predicted that Ken would win his very next tournament start.

His reaction: "That's great! My next event would be the Tournament of Champions in January to start the 1986 season."

However, he was forgetting his commitment to the King Hassan Trophy at Dar Es Salam Golf Club in Morocco a few weeks away. He had considered withdrawing because of all the unrest in the Middle East, but Shelley convinced him to go.

"Well, I won the darn thing, wouldn't you know, and now I'm really glad that I went," confirmed Ken. "Besides the prize money, there's this incredible trophy called the Dagger, and it's mine. Every year, the King's jewelers design a new one. Mine has an ivory handle and gold sheath, and it's hand carved. It's encrusted with 44 different rubies, emeralds and diamonds."

Things are looking rosy for Ken Green right about now. With a month of official TOUR events remaining on the 1986 schedule, Ken ranks 21st on the money list with $251,089. He seems at ease with his future.

"I play golf because I love the game of golf," Green said. "But if I didn't have people to share my successes and my occasional failure or two with, it wouldn't mean that much."

He's already begun to contribute something back. Ken has organized a charity pro-am at Richter Park. This year, he invited 20 of his friends from the PGA TOUR to participate. It was an unqualified success, raising more than $35,000 for the local Hanahoe Memorial Children's Clinic.

It's not easy being Ken Green, but some children at the Hanahoe Clinic are very happy that, after so many years, he has never stopped trying. □

CRIME AND PUNISHMENT

The author has been fined 12 times
in his career (not counting what he'll get
for this article). Is he guilty?
You be the judge

BY KEN GREEN

Editor's note: We at GOLF DIGEST *hardly approve of every action taken by the controversial PGA Tour player, Ken Green. It should be clear, however, that not even Ken Green approves wholeheartedly of Ken Green. Rarely do we accept unsolicited manuscripts from unpublished authors, but when Ken faxed us this article, we felt it gave readers an unfiltered look at a man, if not a tour. As to Green's culpability, the reader is free to supply his own verdict.*

As I keep whacking that little white pellet around, a funny thing has happened in my career. Actually, not so funny, not lately, as the fines have been piling up a lot faster than the victories. I reached a dirty-dozen career fines in 1992, versus five wins in my 11 years on the PGA Tour. My personal theme song might be—with apologies to singer Kenny Rogers— "You picked a fine time to fine me, Lucille."

I'd be the first to admit that I deserved some of them, but these last few incidents seem so ridiculous that the injustice of it all has really ticked me off. That's why I decided to take

my case to you, the golfing public.

What irks me is the arbitrary way in which fines are decided. Some players, believe me, are given much more rope to misbehave than others. Fines are based more on what's reported and by whom than on actual wrongdoing. You'll notice that most of my trouble has stemmed from things seen and reported by Joe Perfect-Strangers, based on my (bad) reputation as much as anything. And the appeals process is a farce, with PGA Tour Commissioner Beane Deman as the sole judge and jury and no chance to overturn the original complaint.

I know I can be a schmuck and my own worst enemy by letting off steam in public. I'm a reactor; I don't play the PR game by worrying about how something is going to be perceived by others. Obviously, some people don't like my style or my attitude and that's what gets me in trouble. But I believe you're being hypocritical if you don't say or do what you think. Even though I know I'll probably get flagged again for this article, I want my side of the story to be heard.

So here is a chronology, as best as I

can re-create it, of my life and f You are about to embark on a j ney to the dark side of pro gol buckle up.

June 1983: It started innoc enough in Memphis during my ond year on the tour. I was sto by my future brother-in-law, official Slugger White (he b my brother-in-law when he m my sister and former caddie Sho It had been reported by an player that my caddie at that ti local, had neglected to rake the

Law and disorder:
Ken Green, frequent
offender of public
morality, tries to
plead his case.

ker on the 16th hole. Thus my very first fine was levied. I was $250 poorer but vowed to seek revenge on Mij Orpthe, I think the name was. Ten years later, I'm still seeking him out.

Fines 1, Wins 0.

September 1988: Five years passed before I was fined again, this despite some very questionable behavior on my part. Picture a man deep in the heat of battle. It was the third round of the Canadian Open and I'm right in the thick of it. I was on the 12th

tee, a killer par 3. I chose a 5-iron and struck it *purr*-fect, flagsville. I was smiling inside as the ball headed for the pin, then shock and anger filled my body as the ball flew over the pin and over the green.

In a rare moment of emotional stability I did not say a thing. I elected instead to "flip off" the ball. Unfortunately for me, a sweet old lady watching in West Virginia happened to see it on TV and sent in a videotape of my "obscene gesture" to tour headquarters. At least she could have sent in the swing, too. Even minus

another $250, I came out way ahead of the deal because I did win the tournament.

Fines 2, Wins 3.

March 1989: The third round of the Players Championship was fairly uneventful except for the fact that I three-jacked five times. The last was too much for me to handle, so I gave my putter the old heave-ho into the lake on 18. This was in full view of the spectators, who oohed and aahed, and tour official Arvin Ginn, who didn't. Ginn reported that I threw the putter 20 to 30 yards into the lake, a clear distortion of what happened. I tossed that bad boy at least 40 yards. I dropped $500 this time, but there was a definite side benefit: I never three-jacked with that putter again.

Fines 3, Wins 4.

August 1989: A Rocky Mountain low. Charley Coe, a dignitary on hand for the International, reported that I broke a CBS microphone on No. 9. I would like to make it clear that I barely touched the mike. Am I to be blamed for defective material that was made in Taiwan? I think CBS should buy American. Another $250 down the drain, but that's just the beginning . . . .

Fines 4, Wins 5.

Jack Vickers, tournament honcho at Castle Pines, wrote Deane a lengthy letter saying I used profanity in front of a marshal and a spectator. He also stated that the spectator ripped up his badges and vowed not to return (attaboy). I must admit I did these dastardly things, but you might have done it, too, if you had a 4-iron in your hand for a second shot into a par 5 and then piped it into the woods.

To the insulted spectator, if you ever decide to try us again please call and I will give you some passes and try not to offend you again. The cost of doing business is going up—this one set me back $1,000—but the good news is I go on probation with my next fine being a three-week vacation.

Fines 5, Wins 5.

April 1990: I was clean until the second round of the Masters. I left a ball hanging on the lip at No. 6, and it proceeded to roll back two inches (nice cup, Hord). Anyway, I proceeded to say, to myself, "Hit the goddam son of a bitch." Trouble. I

Fine No. 7: "Maturity has obviously crept in and I do not fling my putter into the lake. Instead I bury the head of it into the ground."

am reported by a PGA of America official and Deane calls me personally (this must be bad).

Deane asked if I did indeed say this, and I confessed my sin. Deane then told me that if I hadn't used the Lord's name in vain, he would have been able to accept what I said. It's good to know that I can say SOB whenever I please. The commissioner then showed his soft side by saying he's been watching me and because my behavior has improved so much, he's not going to suspend me after all. I'm relieved only of another $500. Too bad; I was looking forward to spending a few weeks in Alcatraz.

Fines 6, Wins 5.

March 1991: Back again at the Players Championship in Ponte Vedra and to the same rotten hole, the par-4 18th, after playing the second nine as my opening nine. Maturity has obviously crept in and I do not fling my putter into the lake this time. Instead I bury the head of it into the ground as I walk to No. 1. Another $500 out of pocket, but at least this time my

caddie was able to fi
putter. But it better be

Fines 7, Wins 5.

April 1991: The lights
out in Georgia but the
aren't. During the
Masters I was reported
buried my putter in
ground as I walked fr
17th to the 18th. I a
doing this but it ce
didn't seem like fine m

Both this fine and the
March were given to me a
same time, and I decided
was time to appeal. I first took
a mini-survey of some player
and asked them if I should b
fined for these actions. Ever
player said the same thing—the
didn't think it was fair, but it's jus
easier to pay up and shut up. I decid
ed to seek out the kings of the bur
ied-and-banged clubs, Lanny [Wad
kins] and Stads [Craig Stadler] fo
their wisdom of experience. Th
conversation went like this:

Ken to Craig: "How many time
have you been fined out here?"

Stads: "Twice."

Ken: "That's all? Thanks."

Ken to Lanny: "How many time
have you been fined in all you
years?"

Lanny: "Once."

Ken: "No way."

I was stunned to find th at thes
guys had escaped relative ely un
scathed while I was piling up fin
and gaining an identity as Pu blic En
emy No. 1. My appeal was o enied.
paid the $500, still steaming.

Fines 8, Wins 5.

December 1991: It's the J[
Classic and I'm paired wi
Bunkowsky in the mixe
event. After the first ro
played decent enough to b
to the pressroom. We playe
empty house of one or two
ers, and press reps from ea
tours. A reporter asked ab
I'm a little different from m